It Works for Me as a Scholar- Teacher

Shared Tips for the Classroom

2

I0221055

Hal Blythe
Foundation Professor of English
Eastern Kentucky University

Charlie Sweet
Foundation Professor of English
Eastern Kentucky University

NEW FORUMS
Stillwater, Oklahoma
U.S.A.

NEW FORUMS PRESS INC.

Published in the United States of America
by New Forums Press, Inc.
1018 S. Lewis St.
Stillwater, OK 74074
www.newforums.com

Library of Congress Cataloging-in-Publication Data Pending

This book may be ordered in bulk quantities at discount from New Forums Press, Inc., P.O. Box 876, Stillwater, OK 74076 [Federal I.D. No. 73 1123239]. Printed in the United States of America.

International Standard Book Number: 1-58107-148-5

Cover design by Katherine Dollar.

Table of Contents

Acknowledgements

We would like to thank our Editorial Assistants, Ben Forsyth and Wendy Schwitters. Without their valuable assistance, this book would never have seen the light of day.

Preface

Hard to believe that it's been ten years since the appearance of our first book in this series, *It Works for Me!* (1998). When we started out, we were just going to publish a soft-cover one-shot containing a few tips on teaching, but our one book turned into a collection that proved so popular we started churning out sequels faster than Hollywood. Actually, "churning out" is far from *le seul mot juste* because we and our contributors have put a lot of thought into the advice we've offered this past decade. And after this book, we have ideas for at least three more.

Our purpose in this book remains the same as that of the first—to provide "a collection of practical tips drawn from real-life experiences." However, our sources have expanded. In the first book we drew from only Kentucky institutions of higher learning, but in this latest collection we present advice from across the country. We want to thank all our contributors, especially the attendees of the Lilly Conference on College Teaching, for sending us such a wide scope and high quality of tips.

It Works for Me as a Scholar-Teacher is divided into two main sections. In the book's first part we bring together some essays and tips on how you can enhance your personal scholarship, whether you're just starting out or have experienced some success as a scholar. The entries explore personal scholarly growth from the more theoretical "Developing a Scholarly Frame of Mind" to the very practical "The Business of Scholarship."

The book's second part offers advice on sharing with students what very effective scholars have learned about theory and practice. In this section you'll find everything from suggestions on how to enhance students' critical thinking to tips on working collaboratively with students on research projects and fostering proper research skills. Appropriately, for this part of the book, we have received tips that do more than just provide basic utilitarian information—this collection includes some theory underlying their practical advice as well as reports on assessment.

In putting together this collection, we've employed several guidelines we've used throughout the "It Works for Me" series. First, because our submissions come from many different disciplines, we have retained the documentation systems used by each contributor. Second, following Henry James' dictum that artists should be granted their artistic *donee*, we have not imposed any stylistic rubrics on the contributors. As a result, some tips are more formal than others. Finally, a confession: while not making any substantive changes, as dyed-in-the-wool English teachers, we've tweaked some contributors' grammatical constructions.

We believe that these tips will be useful in your personal scholarship and your teaching of scholarly theory and methodology. Some advice you can utilize intact, some you can build on, and some you may reject. As Sir Francis Bacon wrote so many years ago, "Some books are meant to be tasted, others to be swallowed, and some few to be chewed and digested."

We hope *It Works for Me as a Scholar-Teacher* offers you a fine meal that stays with you a long time.

INTRODUCTION

The Essentiality of Academic Research

Academic research is essential in moving an institution forward in its efforts to serve its students and the larger community. Whether that research seeks to add to our body of knowledge and to discover and record more of ourselves and our surroundings or it serves to prepare for the next academic term's classroom teaching and course lectures, research must be an elemental part of what happens at a college or university.

Now that you have picked up this book, we know that you are interested in academic research. In fact, if you have taught a class successfully, if only just once, you have *done* research. Your study of the materials you were to teach, examination of how those materials relate to the larger subject area, and at least a basic review of the literature were necessary to get you through that first successful experience. And we know that you want to learn how others use research in their successful experiences.

So, given that you have some feeling for how you experience the value of academic research, let me share some of my experience of how your dean, provost, and president also value it as a part of the fabric of your institution. I have served in each of these administrative positions, so I can speak directly about the views from those chairs. Let me focus on the attitudes of the campus president, who will in the best of worlds provide leadership and example for deans and the provost or chief academic officer as to the role and value of research.

A good university president comes to the office every day hoping to find a new idea, a novel approach, an improved technique, a more effective way to fulfill the academic responsibilities of the institution. And a good university president understands that however eager he or she is to work personally toward those ends, most of the new ideas, improved techniques, and more effective methods come from faculty and staff colleagues through their research activities at various levels. To the extent that these activities happen, the faculty, staff, and president are working together to bring student and institutional success. And this partnership is a good thing.

If your institution includes traditional tenure-track opportunities, doubtless part of the expectations of that process and review is research. Over the last several years, I'm happy to say, more institutions have moved away from the old prejudices and separations of "pure research" and "applied research" and have recognized that research focusing directly on the teaching environment brings strong rewards to all concerned. So we have seen increased effort to bring undergraduate students into research efforts well beyond the traditional term paper assignment, for example.

Research, almost regardless of its focus and type, is an essential part of good teaching. It is vital to both faculty and students in its support and strengthening of both teaching and learning. It enriches the content of the curriculum and the ways in which that curriculum is communicated. Any good academic administrator, including the president, values research as a part of what comes from a quality faculty.

We find ourselves now in a time of lean budgets and reduced resources, so in very practical ways the enhanced knowledge and improved methods resulting from research can enable the institution to preserve its abilities to succeed. And let's not think for a moment that the time ever will come when we are able to say that our resources—human, financial, or otherwise—are sufficient. The value of research in maintaining institutional abilities is a constant.

So in a continuing and strengthening manner, academic research is seen as a public and an institutional good. But at the same time I suggest that your involvement in research should be in part for your own personal and professional good. The personal value of research is a result of its ability to enhance your imagination, your personal confidence, your basic ability to think and to organize better. These elements surely provide improved experiences for your students (and your colleagues). But take a moment to be selfish enough to understand that if you don't experience them, you won't be able to pass them along to anybody.

To return to that crass but oh so necessary element of budgets and finance, it isn't just the major research grants and contracts that build the reputation of academic programs and institutions, resulting in fiscal benefits. Alumni memories (and the financial support that grows from them) always center on the faculty and staff who had the imagination, confidence, and enthusiasm to pass to their students. And in these cases it often doesn't matter whether the research at the base of it all was to find water on Mars or to venture out "simply" to keep classroom experiences fresh and alive.

The "It Works For Me" book you are holding in your hands presents ideas and methods that you should consider. Like the others in *The New Forums Better Teaching Series*, it requires that you interpret and adapt the materials you read. And you would be wise to share it and discuss it with your colleagues—your teacher community or network.

In my own discussions, I talked with my son, Dr. Les Burns of the University of Kentucky's Department of Curriculum and Instruction, who is daily involved in research of the kind we are considering here. What developed is what I see as a valuable summary of how to use *It Works for Me as a Scholar-Teacher*. I mentioned earlier that presidents always are looking for good ideas, and I found good ideas in what he said. I'm passing them along to you as he wrote them:

For the last decade at least, many educators have come to talk in terms of "best" teaching practices based on "scientific" research. But few teachers and researchers really stop to think about what those terms mean, and fewer consider how complex it really is to do good research or to be a high-quality teacher. People want to hear about what is "effective." That's understandable. But the actual definition of "effectiveness" is predictability—if I try Teaching Technique X, will I get the same results in every case every time? The answer to that last question, based on a century of education research and scholarship is, in nearly all cases, "no." Unfortunately, there is no such thing as a "best" practice without asking, "Best for whom? Where? When? Why? How?" Scientific research helps answer these questions, but it has never been able to offer many absolute answers where teaching and learning are concerned. "Science" is an extremely broad term, and in the context of education research it really means *careful and systematic.*

None of this is to say that research-based teaching techniques referred to as "best practices" have no value and should be thrown out. To the contrary; the work and examples contained in texts like the "It Works for Me" series are important. These ideas get professionals thinking about their work in new ways. They provide designs that we can take away and tailor to meet the needs of our students in their unique circumstances. We take these ideas and re-design them to make activities that work for us. One of the first things I tell my own students—people working to become teachers themselves—is that teachers "steal" ideas constantly from research and from each other. Piracy is a virtue, and when someone else "steals" an idea and uses it to help students learn, it is among the highest compliments a teacher or researcher ever gets. *It Works for Me as a Scholar-Teacher* is a bank of knowledge begging to be robbed.

What matters most about any given teaching approach is that it is based on some kind of thoughtful, systematic inquiry—some kind of research. Contrary to current federal definitions of "scientific" research as only and always a matter of controlled experiments, the fact is that experiments in education research cannot ever be fully controlled. Students in classrooms are not rats in mazes. Even so, education is a young field where researchers have made remarkable progress toward understanding the incredible complexities of how people learn. Through case studies, ethnographies, statistical analyses, and, yes, experiments, we have generated a deep body of work describing the incredible diversity of human thought and experience. But quality teaching and high student achievement are almost never products or randomized "scientific" experimentation by itself.

For good reason teaching has been called both an art and a science; it simply defies categories. My personal take on the matter is an infuriating, "It depends." Quality teaching and learning are products of deep thinking about particular learners in specific places who need special attention. Sometimes experimental and statistical data exist that I can use to guide my classroom practices. Sometimes—more often, really—understanding how I can teach best requires me to study other cases and related examples very hard and then adapt them to my classroom in ways I predict will be helpful for my students, or for me. Like it or not, every class we teach every day is different. Time of day matters. When and if the students ate lunch matters! Cultural diversity (or lack of it) matters. So if we want to do our best, our first job is to step back and think about how resources like this book can be used to the full benefit of *this* group in *this* time and *this* place for *this* reason.

Many people look upon the broad field of education "research" with too much suspicion. We often believe that because "it worked for me" that it will work for everybody, and when it doesn't, we conclude that the research must have been done by some ivory-tower hack who doesn't understand the realities of everyday classrooms. But education does not work that way. If you have ever written a lesson plan, watched it work perfectly in second period, and then seen it crash and burn in fifth period after lunch, then you might understand.

It Works for Me as a Scholar-Teacher is an invaluable resource. Its contents are all examples of local research, and every time you steal an idea from it, you become a researcher yourself, trying to find out if an idea will work for you, too. As a teacher-researcher, think hard about how and why you are using one way instead of another. Your teaching will improve because of it, and so will your students. Take this research, work for it, and make it "work for you."

Robert Burns
Retired

Les Burns
University of Kentucky

I. ENHANCING YOUR PERSONAL SCHOLARSHIP

At the end of Tennyson's "Ulysses," the aged warrior exhorts his former mariners "To strive, to seek, to find, and not to yield." Perhaps we're overly romantic, but our view of the scholar is aptly defined by the ancient Greek hero. A scholar is a person who is driven to search for new knowledge, to uncover it, and to persist in this quest no matter what the obstacles. Our experience has been that at their core most true scholars possess a powerful internal motivation that rivals heroes from Ulysses to Indiana Jones "to follow knowledge like a sinking star."

Some beginning scholars have the desire, but don't know where to start. Some seasoned scholars who have been on the quest, like traditional heroes, need help from various guides. Think of this section, then, as a blind hermit, a fool on the hill, or a lady of the lake offering advice to help heroes achieve their goals. Some of the advice tends toward the more abstract and theoretical like the kernel of knowledge contained somewhere in a story from Eastern philosophy, while other tips are more direct, succinct, and practical like the Proverbs.

The essays begin by establishing a definition of what we like to call "a scholarly frame of mind"—i.e., preparing for the scholarly quest. The next section, "Establishing the Boundaries of Scholarship," functions as a summons for your intellectual quest. Finally, "Strategies for Scholarly Work" provides you with five categories of the basic skills necessary to achieve the holy grail of personal scholarship, publication.

Now, as Yoda, the Jedi master, would say, "Do or do not. There is no try."

Developing a Scholarly Frame of Mind

Transforming Yourself Into A Scholar

One morning last year while Charlie was getting dressed, his wife had the TV on, where the host was interviewing one of the Heath brothers about his recent book. Although Charlie was concentrating more on not missing a belt-loop, he managed to overhear enough to suggest that *Made to Stick* sounded interesting. He ordered it from Amazon.com, read it the next weekend, and passed it on to Hal. A few days later over coffee and doughnuts, two sure-fire stimulants, we decided that the book, which focuses on why some commercials and political campaigns gain public traction, could be effectively applied to better teaching. As a result, when we're not writing this book, we've been working on that article.

Why were we able to go from the glimmer of an idea to the scholarly process so quickly and efficiently? Somewhere during our combined seventy-five years as tenure-track faculty our internal drives, our experience in teaching and writing, and books like this one mixed and mingled in our heads to produce in each a scholarly frame of mind.

Despite their ardors and rigors, America's graduate schools do not necessarily produce scholars. In fact, many Ph.D. candidates view the doctoral dissertation the way many of our students treat first-year course term papers—just another academic hurdle to be cleared to reach the degree. As a result, when new graduates are hired into their first instructional position, they have as much chance of attaining the holy trinity of excellence in teaching, scholarship, and service as the knights of the round table did of finding the holy grail.

Scholarship does not come to you like an unbidden muse, nor is it conferred on you by Professor Merlin, who at your Ph.D. degree ceremony places a cowl over your head, touches you with a magic wand, and dubs thee scholar. A scholarly frame of mind is something attained over the years through a deliberate process in which YOU transform yourself from a mere student to a practicing scholar.

What is a scholarly frame of mind? To answer a related question—"Why do you write horror stories?"—popular writer Stephen King posited that he had developed a "filter," a state of mind wherein he paid attention to and absorbed the terrifying events around us. He relates how while teaching high school English one year, he had been observing the coming-of-age rituals going on all around him while reading an article in *Life* magazine on telekinesis; as a result, his filter produced *Carrie.*

Here's another way to look at what we're trying to explain; bear with us, as we are both creative writers and scholars, poets and mathematicians as Poe's Dupin would describe us. In *The Paper Chase,* Harvard law students have the reason they undergo the law school experience described to them by Contracts professor Charles W. Kingsfield, Jr: "You teach yourselves the law. I train your minds. You come in here with a skull full of mush, and if you survive, you'll leave thinking like a lawyer."

A scholarly frame of mind then? How about "thinking like a scholar" as in the circular definition that a "scholar is one who thinks like a scholar"?

Our former dean of Eastern Kentucky University's College of Arts & Sciences, Dr. Andrew Schoolmaster, offers this more academic description: "A scholarly frame of mind is not necessarily defined by one's holding of an advanced degree. Rather it is characterized by attitudé and predisposition to seek understanding, knowledge, and, if possible, the truth about the subject in question. Possibly, a scholarly frame of mind cannot be defined in a traditional sense at all, but is demonstrated by a person's respect for, curiosity about, pursuit of, and passion to practice their craft to the best of their ability."

Perhaps we can find some common characteristics in all these attempts to define that elusive condition and add a few more. A scholarly frame of mind:

- Demonstrates expertise in a field (and often beyond)
- Is self-motivated
- Strives for excellence
- Seeks synthesis/innovation
- Desires proof/causality
- Produces significance.

The purpose of this book, quite frankly, is to provide you with techniques and strategies you can use to develop a scholarly frame of mind and perhaps help foster it in your students. We want to move you from considering scholarship as something you have to do on the side in order to attain promotion and tenure to something that comes naturally, to something you want to do, to something you love, and to something at which you become good. With a true scholarly frame of mind, you do it because you can't conceive of not doing it.

In other words, you come into this book not necessarily with a mind of mush, but you leave thinking like a scholar.

True scholarship is a web involving many aspects. This book seeks to offer you a synthesis of practical ways to attain the desired metamorphosis. To be honest, we want you to be more than a thinking scholar—i.e., a publishing scholar. For some ivory tower scholars, studying, thinking, and discovering the new are sufficient; in academia that scholarship must be demonstrated in the arena of publishing as well as in the classroom. A truly effective (and retained and promoted) scholar not only displays expertise, is extremely self-motivated, strives for excellence, seeks synthesis/innovation, desires proof/causality, and produces something of significance, but also demonstrates these traits in public print. A truly effective scholar is eager to join the scholarly conversation and to insert his/her ideas into the marketplace where they can be tested, challenged, refined, modified, and especially accepted.

Nobody remembers a great thinker like J. J. Newberry, but everybody has been affected by Darwin, Taine, Freud, and Jung. In fact, in the séance of scholarship, we converse with them daily.

If you want some practical advice on joining the conversation and self-growth, read on.

Hal Blythe
Charlie Sweet
Eastern Kentucky University

A Two-Way Street: The Relationship of Scholarship and Teaching

During our nearly 35 years of collaboration, we have published over 100 critical and pedagogical pieces with one thing in common: each was the product of material we were teaching in a class. Sometimes the idea evolved from research into a story for an Am Lit class; sometimes it came from a student comment in creative writing; and sometimes it sprang from a remark one of us made while team-teaching a graduate seminar involving literary theory. Regardless, we always draw from our classes since we long ago realized several benefits to both our teaching and our scholarship.

Our teaching makes us stronger scholars. By working with materials we actually teach, we are afforded an opportunity to bounce ideas off our classes, to in a sense get a dry run with an informed and critical audience. Admittedly the feedback is much stronger in a graduate seminar than in a sophomore class, but often a question coming from a critically naïve underclass student will spark an idea that will take us in a new direction in our research. Additionally, writing about material we're teaching gives us a fuller context for that material. For instance, if we're working on a piece treating Bobbie Ann Mason's use of flight imagery in "Shiloh," we can study her technique within the context not only of her canon, but also the works of other writers we've studied in depth in class.

Likewise, our scholarship makes us more effective teachers. Going beyond a surface approach to the material not only provides us with the obvious deeper insight into what we're teaching, but it also gives us confidence in presenting the material. It's gratifying to watch the ramped-up interest on students' faces when they realize that those guys talking to us about water imagery in Cheever's "The Swimmer" have actually published an article or two on the subject or what they're telling us about the functions of setting in a piece of fiction just appeared in this month's *The Writer* under their byline.

One other argument we make about the benefits of our scholarship is currency. Our doing the research on classroom works keeps up up-to-date on the scholarship. We can not only frame sides in scholarly debates, but we can let our students know what the latest word is. Without the research, we doubt we would even know how the critical armies are lined up on the battlefield. Current research on critical thinking identifies the ability to see opposing viewpoints and to analyze their claims as important. Without the scholarship, we wouldn't be able to do so, nor would we be models for our students in considering and analyzing alternatives.

We are quite aware that Maryellen Weimer in *Enhancing Scholarly Work on Teaching & Learning* (San Francisco: Jossey Bass, 2006) claims that "There is no relationship between research and teaching" (169), but that "Doing pedagogical research does make you a better teacher" (170). Obviously, while we agree with her latter statement, we take issue with her former for some of the reasons we have outlined. In fact, we think more research needs to be done into the areas of currency, critical thinking, and modeling as they contribute as part of the symbiotic scholarship-teaching relationship.

Truthfully, we can't imagine teaching without scholarship or scholarship divorced from the classroom since they have been so mutually supportive through the years.

Hal Blythe
Charlie Sweet
Eastern Kentucky University

Becoming Great at Scholarship

Some people have the work ethic instilled in them as a way of achieving excellence. Do you remember being told, "If it's worth doing at all, it's worth doing well"? In the area of scholarship, not everyone is self-motivated or even wants to be great, and we've heard some defeatist statements. "Scholars are born, and I don't have the talent for it" is one such prevalent attitude. Another is "I tried it for a while, and it didn't work." Then, there's "I do it off and on, but it doesn't seem to get me anywhere." And, "I'm too old for scholarship."

In "What It Takes to be Great" that appeared in the 30 October 2006 issue of *Fortune* (pp. 88+), researchers expose these attitudes as myths and suggest what it takes to become an excellent scholar.

First, research has demonstrated that "targeted natural gifts don't exist" (88). No one is born with the natural talent of a scholar. If so, our high school term papers would have been published by now.

Second, research has discovered that "nobody is great without work" (89). As in most fields, practitioners learn quickly at first, then slow down. In fact, there is "no evidence of high-level performance without experience or practice" and that "even the most accomplished people need around ten years of hard work before becoming world class" (89). Think about the ten-year rule in relation to tenure and promotion to full professor at most universities. Doesn't it take about a decade to receive this rank and privilege?

Third, sporadic habits and performances don't get the job done. To be an excellent scholar necessitates what experts call "deliberate practice ... activity that's explicitly intended to improve performance, that reaches for objectives just beyond one's level of competence, provides feedback on results, and involves high levels of repetition" (94). See our piece on "The Decalogue of Scholarly Discipline."

Fourth, not all scholars/practitioners develop in their fields at the same rate. Chemists and theoretical economists tend to peak in their mid-thirties, data-driven economists in their mid-fifties, and philosophers in their mid-sixties. Furthermore, in "many fields (music, literature) elite performers need 20 or 30 years' experience before hitting their zenith" (89).

What the research demonstrates, then, is that to become good, even excellent, at research, you have to do it every day for a long time and you must do it right. You can get lucky early—Charlie, for instance, sold the first article he ever wrote for *TV Guide*, but hasn't sold one to the magazine since; of course, he didn't work at it. As we relate in another piece, we wrote 24 short mysteries for *Ellery Queen's Mystery Magazine* before selling our first, which was good perseverance but not good practice. Why? Because we weren't writing the right way.

Years ago we learned a valuable lesson from an old Little League coach: "Practice doesn't make perfect—perfect practice makes perfect." But only, coach should have added, if you practice a long time! Adhering to that advice probably explains why we were able to average 20 publications per year over a twenty-year span.

Excelsior!

Hal Blythe
Charlie Sweet
Eastern Kentucky University

———————————————

What About that Coonskin Cap?
Scholarship at a Teaching Institution-
The Art of Integration

The comprehensive regional university where I teach prides itself on being a teaching institution. Our history begins as Eastern Kentucky Normal School dedicated to the training of teachers; we became a four-year institution in 1922 with the name Eastern Kentucky Normal School and Teachers College, renamed the Eastern Kentucky State Teachers College in 1930, and only in 1948 was the reference to teachers removed from the name and the institution certified to grant nonprofessional degrees. Yet today, pride in teaching well is pervasive, and the college of Education and its teacher-training mission remain at the heart of the university. The University's current mission statement says we are "student centered" and lists instruction first in higher education's common triumvirate of teaching, scholarship, and service. In recent years the University marketed itself as the school "where students come first." Administrators have backed the teaching emphasis by funding a Teaching & Learning Center. Our newly-inaugurated president insisted in his speech that "Teaching is job one." We promote faculty learning communities, and we run a laboratory school. And for twenty-five years I have felt fulfilled in my role of teacher.

Recently, however, I had occasion to revisit a text I taught regularly to freshmen some twenty years ago, *Zen and the Art of Motorcycle Maintenance: An Inquiry into Values* by Robert M. Prirsig. The book developed something of a cult following on college campuses in the 1980's. At my university we sent paperback copies to incoming students in the Honors Program and discussed the book, chapter by chapter, in a one – credit orientation course. The book is structured on the age-old theme of a journey, in this case a motorcycle trip that the author takes with his eleven-year old son. And like other epic journeys from the *Odyssey to Huck Finn*, the characters learn more about themselves as they travel than they learn about the places they visit en route. The events of the trip prompt an exploration not only outward, but inward as well. Father and son have the leisure to repair their relationship, to explore their individual identities, and to question the meaning of life. In reading the book with my students in the 80's, we talked about such heady topics as the nature of creativity and logical reasoning, of the use of spontaneity and the difference between art and craft, of work and leisure, and how all these things fit together to make a centered human being and a coherent world view.

In reviewing the book this time, however, I happened upon a passage that I didn't remember. The narrator recalls a time when he was a teacher. He writes about the school where he taught and what it was like to teach there:

The school was what could euphemistically be called a "teaching college." At a teaching college you teach and you teach and you teach with no time for research, no time for contemplation, no time for participation in outside affairs. Just teach and teach and teach until you mind grows dull and your creativity vanishes and you become an automaton saying the same dull things over and over to endless waves of innocent students who cannot understand why you are so dull, lose respect and fan this disrespect out into the community. The reason you teach and you teach and you teach is that this is a very clever way of running a college on the cheap while giving a false appearance of genuine education. (Pirsig 147)

Ouch!

Surely Pirsig cannot be describing my university, or worse yet, describing me! But just as surely, we are teaching institution. The normal course load is four courses each semester. Lecturers teach five courses one semester and four the next. "You teach and you teach and you teach," Pirsig writes. For twenty-five years I have taught at least four courses a semester, sometimes taking on an overload to boost a weak salary or without compensation to save a threatened program. Unfortunately, my situation is not unique. My institution is not unique. One year of such a heavy teaching load is one thing, but to perform it year after year and year is something different again. Nathaniel Hawthorne knew the difference, and wrote about it in *The Scarlet Letter* when he contrasted Hester Prynne's ordeal of standing on the scaffold wearing her scarlet letter with the different burden occasioned by her release from prison and resumption of normal life:

> [Standing on the scaffold] was [. . .] a separate and insulated event , to occur but once in her lifetime, and to meet which, therefore, reckless of economy, she might call up the vital strength that would have sufficed for many quiet years. [. . .] But now [. . .] began the daily custom, and she must either sustain and carry it forward by the ordinary resources of her nature, or sink beneath it. She could no longer borrow from the future to help her through the present grief.[. . .] The days of the far-off future would toil onward [;. . .] the accumulating days and added years would pile up their misery upon the heap of shame. (74)

Not that I wish to compare teaching with the punishment for adultery! But Hester's sense of weariness, of disappointment, and maybe even of shame carry over to our profession when we realize the extent to which teaching usurps research at a teaching institution. And so I will confess to sometimes resenting the missionary zeal of job applicants with their newly minted Ph.D.'s interviewing for our low-paying positions, seeing in their naïve idealism shard of myself at the beginning of my career, haunting me as Pirsig's Phaedrus, his prior self, haunts him on his present journey. The possibility that Prisig might be right—that after so much teaching, there is no time for research, as "your mind grows dull and your creativity vanishes"—terrifies the veteran teacher at a teaching institution. If Prisig is right, I don't want to know it.

So how is the veteran teacher to keep Pirsig's analysis from becoming prophecy? How can someone with such a heavy teaching load as is common at my university and many like it, continue to keep intellectually alive, and not bore students with ideas generated decades ago? For me, the answer has been the challenge of constantly learning new things—either in my field or in the field of teaching and learning. Not only does scholarship keep the individual alive, but it keeps the classroom vital as well.

Yet with very little time, scholarship cannot follow the determined and careful path pursued by our graduate instructors in research institutions, faculty who teach one or possibly two courses, keep minimum office hours, and hold their research time absolutely sacrosanct. Time is in high demand at a teaching institution, but administrators and students neither encourage an individual faculty member nor condone it if he/she hordes research time. So one learns to rely on different strategies. And here is my tip for conducting research at a teaching institution: use as much as possible the business of one's professional life, including special teaching moments and faculty development opportunities, as the centerpiece of one's scholarship. Bring your scholarship into your classroom, and let the sparks from the classroom light the way to your research and writing.

Let me give you an example of a project that has revitalized several of the courses I teach, supported one research project, and given birth to another. I teach a basic, chronologically structured, freshman and sophomore Humanities course for the Honors Program. Because coverage is crucial and chronological structure mandated, there is little room for invention in course design, and the material of the course is outside my field of expertise—all of this a prime recipe for the disastrous intellectual life Pirsig laments. However, the Honors programs in the various public Kentucky universities get together once a semester, and the National Collegiate Honors Council holds an annual conference; both venues provide opportunities for students to share the results of their research. Since I teach freshmen and sophomores, if they wish to present at a conference, they need considerable mentoring, especially to participate in the national conference. Generally the theme of the national conference is very broad. The theme for next year, for example is the frontier. My tip here is to advise teachers to seize upon such a situation and to identify something you would like to learn about and possibly write about. If you show some excitement about your topic, there are generally some students who will take the bait and join you in your research endeavors.

Situated near the Cumberland Gap and almost within throwing distance of Fort Boonesborough, Eastern Kentucky University has a stature of Daniel Boone as a landmark on the campus. Surprisingly, few students know much about Boone. They rub the toe of his shoe for good luck on an exam, but no one yet has even conducted an experiment to confirm whether or not the lore holds up! Because of our general ignorance about the man whose identity has prompted a living history museum and whose name announces businesses and social service agencies alike in our area, I proposed a panel for the National Collegiate Honors Council conference on the myths and historical truths about Daniel Boone. The topic generated considerable interest among the students, and I had more students volunteering to work on the project than I could accept. We met outside of class to discuss what we knew or thought we knew about the historical figure. Each student chose some aspect of the Boone legend to research: his clothing, his gun, where he lived, his family relationships, his personality, his activity in war, his education, and so on. We looked at elements of popular culture (the television series, cartoons, and pictures) and compared the "myth" to what historians tell us. Focusing on those areas between popular myth and historical reality that are most disparate, we presented our findings at one of the state-wide meetings of Honors programs, conceiving the presentation as preliminary to the national conference.

All of this sounds like "teaching," not research. True. These undergraduates are learning a good deal, not only about specific historical figure and the time period that he lived in, and about popular culture and how legends and myths play a role in society, but also about the processes and expectations involved in preparing for academic conferences. But I am learning, too. As a faculty member in Humanities, I do not often have the opportunity to do research with students or to have students carry out my research agenda. Yet this is one time when I can do just that. Because I am working with a small group of students, I can send them off to research one small segment of the project, and because they are new at doing research, they accept my suggestions on *how* to do this research as I point them in the direction of discipline-specific databases and appropriate professional journals, moving them away from using Google as their primary source. When we bring our information together or post it online in a special Blackboard site, peer pressure kicks in to accomplish the assigned research task in order to be able to contribute to creating an informative panel presentation.

As it turns out, the original source of information about Boone appeared in Jon Filson's *The Discovery, Settlement, and Present State of Kentucky* (1784). "The Adventures of Colonel Daniel Boon" was published as an appendix to Filson's history and presented as Boone's autobiography. I teach an excerpt from this work in one of my courses, an upper division class on Kentucky Literature. Whatever I can learn about the real Boone and about how popular culture has represented and misrepresented him will help me in teaching Filson's excerpt in my course. Note that the impact of this research is far removed from the freshman Honors survey class whose students are engaged in this research. With majors in everything from Safety Management to Journalism, elementary education to forensic biology, it is unlikely that a single one of these students will take my upper division English course. Nevertheless, they are learning, and I am stretched as well, for I too need new information to bring back to the group, new directions to encourage the students to pursue, and new insights to bring to the material in my expertise. Thus it is that teaching prompts scholarship, which feeds back into better teaching.

As these students analyze popular myth and probe for historical truth, they are learning how to conduct research, the limits of internet searches, the difference between myth and history, the nature of academic journals, how to evaluate internet sites, and so on. While these research skills are probably the most important aspect of the exercise for them, for me it is the result of their findings-the content itself, that is most important. The content is the research I do not have time to conduct by myself in a teaching institution, but which will certainly be useful the next time I teach Filson's history in my Kentucky Literature course.

But even more interesting is how this work on Boone relates to two other research projects-one indirectly and one directly. For some time I have been pursuing the writing of William Clark, the Kentucky half of the Lewis and Clark Expedition. Approximately twenty-five years after Daniel Boone developed Fort Boonesborough, William Clark would take his slave, York, and leave the Falls of the Ohio at Louisville, Kentucky, heading west en route with Meriwether Lewis on the most famous epic American journey of all time, eventually reaching the Pacific Ocean, but on a much more difficult track than anyone had anticipated. I have been reading Clark's journals, trying, among other things, to identify distinctive features of his work and to determine the degree to which Clark was shaped by the Kentucky frontiersman myth personified in Daniel Boone. Seemingly tangential to my study of the writings of Clark, my own and my students' research on Boone helped me identify changes in the perceived landscape and in the socio-political conditions of "America" a quarter century later. An essay on Clark is in the hands of an editor waiting for reviews from readers.

The second influence is more direct. Research with students on Boone has now prompted me to take a deeper look at Filson's account of the man and the literary strategies used in the "autobiography." I am now better equipped to understand Filson's early literary text on Boone in the specific context of their time. That is, I can identify Filson's rhetorical distortions and assess both Filson's rhetorical and Boone's historical contexts. In terms of enhancing direct productivity as a scholar, I am writing a critical analysis of Filson's "The Adventures of colonel Daniel Boon." Engaging students in research enhances both my teaching and my scholarship.

The tip to be gained from the example I have described is really quite simple: at a teaching institution, use the "teaching moment" creatively to energize your teaching and to enrich, deepen, and jumpstart your own research. Integrate as much as possible the students' scholarship and your own research interests. Let the results of your research impact what you teach and how you teach it, and in this way you share your research with as many students as possible. At a teaching institution, perhaps at any institution, scholarship may lead you down unpredictable paths. Enjoy the journey, and make the most of the trip.

And by the way, Daniel Boone did *not* wear a coonskin cap. And his Kentucky rifle was made in Pennsylvania.

References

Hawthorne, Nathaniel. *The Scarlet Letter.* New York: Bedford Books, 1991.

Pirsig, Robert M. *Zen and the Art of Motorcycle Maintenance: An Inquiry into Values.* (1974) New York: William Morrow, 1999.

Paula Kopacz
Eastern Kentucky University

Work from the Center Outward

As a teacher of interdisciplinary humanities with an emphasis in world literature and a background in music (instrumental and choral performance and conducting), I found it difficult in the early years of my career to decide where to direct my efforts as a scholar. For the first eight years of that career I was an English teacher at a large community college, where teaching was the *sine qua non* and scholarship was what you could do between the cracks with a regular schedule of five classes (three composition classes and two world literature classes usually). It seemed then that my Ph.D in interdisciplinary humanities with a dissertation in Shakespeare and Renaissance Neo-Platonism had receded into a relatively distant dimension. My Master's degree in English, with a thesis in modern poetry, served as a more useful field of knowledge for the classes I was teaching. I read widely during those eight years, developed a course in Oriental Literature, absorbed all the fiction and poetry of 20th century European, Asian, African, and Latin American contemporaries that I could find in translation, and presented short papers at small conferences, since my meager salary and small institutional support did not allow me to attend the larger conventions.

When I moved to a regional university with an interdisciplinary humanities curriculum, I found, to my surprise, that conditions were not very different from those at the community college. Again, I was engaged in a heavy teaching load: four classes per semester, but with a larger number of students per class, such that the teaching and grading load was actually more, not less. As for institutional support for travel, there was a little more but not enough to make a difference; I was actually twenty years into my teaching career before my salary reached a level high enough to afford to invest in my own scholarship. But I had developed a strategy to maintain both my own interest and productivity in the face of what were, in retrospect, severe odds. I had learned to work from the center outward.

At the heart of any scholar's work there must be a first love, a center of intellectual being, a starting point from which a design may grow outward. The paradigm I have in mind originates, I believe, in Emerson's observation that "The eye is the first circle," from which consciousness emanates outward to the horizon and then on to the universe. We are all, individually, at the center of our intellectual and existential universe. From there we work outward, in Whitman's terms, "seeking the spheres to connect them." For me, this center was Shakespeare. Shakespeare and the Renaissance were and are my original scholarly foundation; I teach the plays regularly, even in general education classes, and write Shakespeare articles from time to time, to return to this home. From Shakespeare, moving outward, I have developed interests in modern literature, both poetry and the novel, which are broadly humanistic and which follow the arc of the Shakespearean premise that human drama, the human story, is both mimetic and existentially redemptive. Epic musical forms, especially the symphony and opera (musical drama) echo this Shakespearean pattern and carry it to the arena of the third circle of Emerson's paradigm, that which is wordless but not without meaning. On this map of concentric circles all of my scholarly pieces of the past 30 years, some 40 or so articles including several on Japanese haiku and short story writers, can be located. What might appear to be a rather widely dissociated series of scholarly pieces to others has for me an organizational principle, one which has proven very useful for me, as I am able to coordinate the works I am teaching with the scholarship I attempt and to make sense of the broad range of genres, art forms, and cultures into which I have ventured. The courses I teach in interdisciplinary humanities, along with honors courses I have developed in the opera and the symphony as cultural narratives, are informed and integrated by the modest scholarship I have undertaken.

Perhaps mine is a special case, as I have for the last fifteen years held a part time administrative position in International Education while teaching two classes, sometimes three, per semester. This situation has further broadened my outlook on people and the cultures they come from, but it has also limited the time I have for scholarship. Nevertheless, I enjoy teaching and would not like to abandon the classroom for full time administration. I feel that working from the center outward has helped me to remain a scholar, if only at a secondary pace, a more informed and better organized teacher, and also a happier person, as I have a view of my own work which is, to me at least, coherent and worthwhile. Those concentric circles noticed by Emerson were, of course, a Neo-Platonic paradigm that has perhaps been reborn in the modern era, one that has antecedents in Hindu mythology and for that matter in a pond where one might drop a stone. Like the Oriental rug in Somerset Maugham's *Of Human Bondage*, though it may be a mere fragment, it contains the pattern of life, or one of many. Everyone is somewhere in that pattern.

Neil H. Wright
Eastern Kentucky University

Establishing the Boundaries of Scholarship

Boyer Plus One and that Equals Fun: Types of Scholarship

In *Scholarship Reconsidered* (1990), Ernest Boyer points out that in 1969 the percentage of university professors responding "Strongly Agree" to the statement "In my department it is difficult for a person to achieve tenure if he or she does not publish" was 21%; by 1989 it was 42% (12). What do you think the percentage is in 2009? Our guess is that it hasn't gone down.

Obviously each year scholarship (once called "research") becomes more and more important for not only surviving in higher ed, but thriving. As a result, one of the first things you need to do to remain on Survivor Island is to check your university's requirements on scholarship. For instance, at Eastern Kentucky University (EKU), the *Faculty Handbook* specifies that "faculty members have an obligation to engage in scholarly activity beyond that required for preparation of classes" (Part V). Of course, your college and department may have even stricter requirements in their promotion, tenure, and evaluation documents. Next, you need to discover your university's definition of scholarship. At EKU, the *Faculty Handbook* continues, "Scholarly activity is defined as research, artistic performance, and creative or technical achievement" (Part V). You might even check out your university's strategic plan to learn the role and significance your school ascribes to scholarship. Our *Eastern Kentucky University Strategic Plan 2006-2010* stresses the importance of scholarship in its mission statement: "Eastern Kentucky University is a student-centered, comprehensive public university dedicated to high-quality instruction, scholarship, and service."

Basically, then, most universities, like Eastern, recognize five types of scholarship— Boyer's four overlapping categories plus one more, creative endeavors. The Boyer model is fairly traditional, but the fifth category sometimes needs champions to keep it from being treated lightly or even dismissed.

The scholarship of discovery, the first Boyer category, is often used as a synonym of research. Discovery includes those endeavors that expand "the stock of human knowledge" (17). Sometimes new information is found, a new product is invented, or a system is created. Most often found in the natural and social sciences, this scholarship provides solid evidence to prove hypotheses and is central to the mission of the university.

The scholarship of integration is often multi-disciplinary, breaking down traditional academic silos by "making connections across the disciplines, placing the specialties in larger context, illuminating data in a revealing way" (18). This scholarship synthesizes, educates people outside a field, and even breaks down traditional barriers.

The scholarship of application moves academia out of its ivy-covered towers and into the street. Involving more than mere participation, this scholarship emphasizes engagement and service wherein intellectual insights are usefully applied to societal problems, serving the community, the nation, and the world.

The scholarship of teaching (and learning), which was not well defined by Boyer, is more than teaching per se. Located in the spectrum with educational research on one end and personal experience in teaching on the other, this scholarship, often called SOTL, seeks to improve student learning. Appreciated less in the natural sciences, SOTL is still in its infancy.

The scholarship of creative endeavor, the outpouring of those most often in the arts and humanities, is sometimes not even recognized as scholarship and was not included in the original Boyer quartet. Yet Boyer recognized that the university was constantly changing, that the writing of textbooks and popular writing "should be recognized as a legitimate scholarly endeavor" (35). In fact, Chapter 4, "The Creativity Contract," contains a chart on "The Height of Creative Powers" (49). At many schools this type of scholarship includes those publications, performances, and technical achievements that evolve from the artistic process. These public results provide new insights into emotion and cognition that help us better apprehend the human condition.

As two who have published literary criticism, SOTL, poetry, and short stories, we have become very much aware of how scholarship informs each one of our works. We strongly disagree with our colleagues outside the arts who contend the field has no "research" to it. For instance, a few years ago we published a piece of fiction in *Ellery Queen's Mystery Magazine* called "Draw Play" that offered readers a humorous insight into the abuses abounding with SSI, Social Security disability insurance. The writing of the short story involved **discovery**—we had to perform traditional research into SSI, **integration**—we had to interweave selected literary conventions with an area of social science, and **application**—we had to place our research and discipline-specific knowledge of literature into a form that could be readily understood by the average American. That we were able to write about using "Draw Play" in our creative writing classes to help students learn how to craft fiction even makes our experience an example of SOTL.

We could point out that Nobel Prizes are given in both science and literature. We could mention that while the *sina qua non* of publication is the peer-reviewed article, art and musical performances are "juried." We could analyze many of our other works that have a strong research base (our "Death of Charety," for instance, necessitated our becoming experts on the founding of Boston, MA). But perhaps the days when Charlie could get passed over for promotion because his works were all in creative writing are truly over, and the scholarship of creative endeavor has won acceptance within the hallowed halls of academia.

Hal Blythe
Charlie Sweet
Eastern Kentucky University

Expanding the Boundaries of Scholarship

Traditional scholarship, no matter the field, looks pretty much the same. Although the sciences rely on proof demonstrated by the scientific method and the arts and humanities stress the value of supported opinion, published articles follow a common pattern of hypothesis, review of criticism/literature, evidence, and conclusion. Admittedly the bibliographic forms vary somewhat because they reflect different mindsets, but most scholarly article writers still feel repeatedly poured into a familiar form. Is it possible to break out, to push the boundaries of scholarship?

We can't vouch for other fields, but in English we found a way to work outside the box. Actually, we were able to accomplish this feat by combining our twin loves, literary criticism and fiction writing into a new genre we created and called **fictional criticism**. Here's how it works.

While most of the time our literary criticism grows out of whatever work we're teaching, back in the early 80s we got stuck in an Edgar Allan Poe groove. At the same time as fiction writers, we were breaking into the popular mystery market with appearances in *Ellery Queen's Mystery Magazine* and *Mike Shayne Mystery Magazine*. We were trying to write an article on what really happened in Poe's short masterpiece "The Fall of the House of Usher," and while we loved the vampire interpretations, we wanted to suggest a more down-to-earth explanation. One day it hit us that Poe had launched the good ship detective story with his creation of the world's first fictional private investigator, C. Auguste Dupin, in a trio of stories in the 1840s. Why did Usher fall? As Dupin himself said in "The Purloined Letter," "Perhaps it is the very simplicity of the thing which puts you at fault."

Our solution? We decided to write a "lost" tale of Dupin wherein the Parisian P.I.

is hired to solve the Usher case. We followed the classical pattern of the short story, invented by Poe himself, but when we came to the convention of the baffled authorities (think puzzled Commissioner Gordon needing the great detective Batman), we inserted the theories of previous literary critics. Thus, this convention covered the important literary criticism characteristic of the review of criticism (calling it the "review of literature" in the field of literature can be confusing). Dupin, of course, was the *raisonneur* for our critical thesis/hypothesis, and his evidence was our support.

In the end this fictional criticism was published in a journal of the Popular Culture Association, *Clues*.

Can other fields break through the boundaries of scholarship? Let us know if you can.

Hal Blythe
Charlie Sweet
Eastern Kentucky University

No Longer the Red-Headed Stepchild: The Emergence of the Scholarship of Teaching & Learning

Since being appointed Co-Directors of our university's Teaching & Learning Center (TLC) and thus assuming a leadership role in professional development on our campus, we have fought hard to establish the scholarship of teaching and learning (SOTL) as a viable pursuit for those seeking to improve their quality of instruction as well as strengthening their promotion and tenure credentials. Even though Ernest Boyer admits SOTL into the pantheon of critical concerns, the majority from instructors through deans around here has been a little less accepting. In a recent survey, less than 10% of faculty even admitted to knowing what SOTL really is, and one administrator-hard scientist commented at a recent roundtable we held to discuss scholarly approaches, "SOTL is something you can do if you can't hack it in real research."

Fortunately, at that same roundtable the dean of the College of Education, a publishing scholar as well as respected teacher, defended SOTL's status, concluding, "How can we claim to be teachers and not respect the scholarship treating the way we teach?" The roundtable ignited a move at EKU to recognize the merits of SOTL along with arriving at a working definition beyond Boyer's limited description.

Perhaps one reason SOTL has had a difficult time becoming a coin of the realm is that ours and other institutions have trouble, like Boyer, defining exactly what it is. For us, SOTL is a vast area that includes the poles of pure educational research and pure personal experience, and it contains these traits:

1. **Published/presented**—i.e., it has appeared in the public arena. As such, it becomes part of the scholarly conversation.

2. **Invites criticism**—i.e., recognizing it is incomplete, it invites others to build upon it.

3. **Purposefully created to improve student learning**—i.e., be it a tip, a tactic, a strategy, an approach, and/or methodology, its ultimate goal is a contribution to student learning.

4. **More than teaching per se**—i.e., teaching is the specific application of more generalized theories of teaching.

5. **Part of an investigative process of discovery** that has as its basis in problems to be solved, practices to be analyzed, questions to be answered, theories to be investigated—i.e., different disciplines will frame it differently.

6. **Represents shared knowledge**—i.e., not only does it build upon other scholarship, but that scholarship may be in other disciplines.

7. **Innovative**—while most often building upon shared knowledge, it recognizes the possibility of untried insight, a bolt from the blue—i.e., the possibility that someone could have a purely eureka moment (n.b., this principle of innovation might be seen as an exception to many of the essential characteristics).

8. **Reveals expertise** that could be in the discipline, the approach, or possibly experience—i.e., it is systematic so that it reflects a recognizable methodology.

9. **Notes sources** where applicable—i.e., demonstrates an awareness of the necessity of proper documentation and research techniques.

10. **Impacts student learning**—i.e., not only does it contribute to student learning, but it provides something to change or with the potential to change teaching/learning somewhere on a continuum from minor to major impact.

Whether coming in the form of tips in books such as ours or more educational research-oriented pieces in the *Journal of Excellence in College Teaching*, SOTL is gaining a new status in the arena of scholarship—one that is long overdue.

Hal Blythe
Charlie Sweet
Eastern Kentucky University

_____

Strategies for Scholarly Work

1. Pre-Writing

The Decalogue of Scholarly Discipline

When Moses came down from the mountain, he brought the wandering tribes a standard for moral conduct. Now we don't claim to be prophets, but we do want to share some writing standards that have certainly profited us. Call them ten timely tips, call them behavioral objectives, or call them The Decalogue of Discipline—but if you call on them as a new habit, be prepared for a transformation from wandering scholar to published author.

Why is discipline so important? Research into scholarly production has determined so few scholars possess this necessary trait. Boice emphasizes this problem by asserting, "the usual incidence of productive scholars within a discipline is less than 15%" (15). Many faculty blame heavy teaching loads, but again Boice points out that "proportionately as many faculty at teaching campuses manage to publish at respectable rates as at research campuses" (17), so obviously these faculty are able to discipline themselves. New faculty seem to be the least productive, spending "0.5 hours per week on manuscript writing" and "producing 0.3 manuscripts during their first two years" (18).

If you want to improve your production, here's our Decalogue:

1. **Determine your scholarly goals.** What is it you're really interested in writing? No matter your discipline, the spectrum is wide. Rather than jumping headlong into some broad, nebulous project—Twentieth Century Female Poetic Theory or Juvenile Drinking—zero in on some specific focus within the larger field, one perhaps that has intrigued you in the past or one that reveals a dearth of scholarship upon it. What questions would you like answered; what problems solved?

2. **Research the area in which you intend to write.** Once you've determined that specific area on which you wish to focus, start your research in systematic fashion. While the Internet can be a dangerous tool, it can provide some foundational information. We've found that the librarians at our university can be extremely helpful in evaluating

web sources as well as pointing us toward relevant databases (here, librarians are assigned to be liaisons and experts for specific departments). And don't forget to seek out those journals that might be interested in your findings. Study their formats to give you a head start regarding submission of your scholarly piece (see also our "Performing Market Analysis").

3. **Set up a work place.** Find a comfortable space of your own where you can write. Some people use a kitchen table, some a carrel in the library, and some find a special booth at a local restaurant. The trick is to get away from the office if possible; there, too many distractions exist.

4. **Establish a specific time.** Try to pick a consistent time that you won't give up for anything. Some prefer to work early before others are awake, while some are night owls, laboring after everyone else sleeps. Whenever, for that period nothing else matters, especially email and the Internet. And try to produce something at every writing session, even if it's not your best work. If you simply say, "I'm going to work for two hours every day from 5:00-7:00 a.m.," you're likely to find yourself sitting down at the computer, staring at the blank screen while thoughts of ungraded papers and unpaid bills flicker across your mind, thereby excusing an unproductive session with "Well, I put in my time today."

5. **Be willing to revise.** An old Hollywood axiom holds that "Nothing is written—everything is rewritten." By beginning every writing session with a rereading and revising of the previous session's work, you'll have a running start at the day. Don't be afraid to prune. The last sacred words were on stone tablets, and even Moses had to go back up the mountain to have them rewritten.

6. **Seek criticism.** Like the long-distance runner, the scholar often feels alone, and one's work is so difficult to judge. You should look for criticism of your work, whether from a spouse, colleague, or writing group. Even if your work is highly specialized, another person might be able to provide insight into your organization, transitions, clarity, or even what a split infinitive is. And don't allow your ego to be so frail that you're unwilling to assess their critiques objectively.

7. **Send your work out.** No scholarship secreted in a closet box has ever been published. Summoning up the nerve to submit a piece is often the hardest aspect to getting started. After all, a jury of your peers is the ultimate critic. Eventually, though, all children must leave the nest, and your only cost has been time. Besides, all peer review is done blindly, so nobody knows your name if you're rejected, and a lot of people learn your name when you are published.

8. **Keep an inventory.** When you begin your career as a productive scholar, you ask yourself as you turn on your email, "How could I ever forget where my manuscript is or how long it's been there?" By your seventh submission, however, you could be in trouble. Keep an inventory (see our "The Business of Scholarship") that details where each article is, when it was submitted, and its current disposition.

9. **Learn from rejection.** Popular writers get rejection slips, and scholars usually receive anonymous review snippets. Some drop rejections in trash cans, some decorate walls with them, and others simply hit "Delete." But there is a much better use. Read each rejection carefully. Was a specific problem mentioned? Was there perhaps a short handwritten note included or a personal comment from an editor? Maybe the editor made some suggestions for revision that if you were willing to take could result in reconsideration. Keep any elaborated rejection with your manuscript for future reference (see our "Beating Rejectionslipitis" for more details).

10. **Keep your manuscripts circulating.** Remember, a baseball player who gets a hit only once every three times at bat is likely to become an All-Star. Perhaps your manuscript was rejected, not for lack of quality or significance, but because the journal was overstocked or had already accepted a piece similar to yours (if the latter, send it to another journal immediately). We recently had a piece that had been to fourteen different publications in twenty-five years—with as many revisions—accepted. Persistence pays off.

Certainly, no sure-fire formula exists for turning you into a published scholar, but the Decalogue will reduce the odds—more than ten-fold.

Reference

Boice, Robert. "Strategies for Enhancing Scholarly Productivity." *Writing and Publishing for Academic Authors.* Ed. Joseph Moxley. Lanham, MD: UP of America, 1996. 15-32.

Hal Blythe
Charlie Sweet
Eastern Kentucky University

Making Time for Research

Like in any other field, research in physics requires a block of time where one can focus exclusively on a particular problem. Most of my research problems require me to be in my office because I need my computer to work on calculations. With my heavy teaching load, however, it can be almost impossible to have an uninterrupted block of time to work on research while in my office. I have been able to solve this problem with proper planning. When I set my office hours at the beginning of each semester, I also set "research hours." The number and duration of the research blocks depend on my teaching schedule for a particular semester. Typically, I schedule two blocks per week and they are between two and four hours long. During my research block, I close my office door, I do not answer the phone, and I only write or respond to research-related e-mail. By experimenting over the years, I have found that it is best for me to schedule these blocks in the afternoons, especially on a Friday. I have also learned that it is important to treat the research blocks as if they are sacred. It is easy to schedule things like committee meetings during those blocks. However, I've had to develop the mindset that I am not "free" during those blocks. I have found that the research blocks have helped me be productive even with a heavy teaching load. I have also noticed that while I may only schedule five hours of research blocks a week, it is not unusual for me to spend up to 10 hours on my research per week. This "extra time" has developed only recently in my career as I have "gotten my classes down" (so to speak) and have learned how to use my time more efficiently.

Christopher Kulp
Eastern Kentucky University

Start Here: Where Do All Those Ideas Come From?

Last year as facilitators of New Faculty Development Day at our institution, we mentioned in passing that we had over 600 publications. One of the group immediately raised her hand to ask the inevitable question that our graduate students have been peppering us with for years: where do you guys find all your ideas?

One answer is still the same: where do you NOT find ideas? Admittedly, we have an advantage in that there are two of us, we are both creative writers and scholars, and as scholars we have two areas of passion, literary criticism and pedagogy. And we have a combined 75 years in the classroom.

Had we been in a graduate class, our answer would have been the same, but rendered more erudite. When a young writer asked Henry James for some advice, he responded, "Try to be one of the people on whom nothing is lost." A recent IBM commercial illustrated James' notion graphically by CGI-ing ideas in the air that flit around the city waiting for people to grab them.

Now if the idea that ideas are everywhere seems too vague, too general, and the kind of answer English teachers seem to love to give, let us be more specific.

Ideas abound in every class you've ever taught. Even in Freshman English. Over the years we've published 15 articles on Bobbie Ann Mason's short story par excellence, "Shiloh," and another 15 on John Cheever's magnum opus, "The Swimmer." The assault on "Shiloh" began because one day in preparing for class we noticed Mason used a lot of bird imagery, which is a fairly common image pattern for female American writers (e.g., Bradstreet, Chopin, Dickinson), and we had to know why. All fictional works read like mysteries to us, and so just to discuss our assignment with our students we've had to figure out why Lardner's Whitey tells the story of an "accidental shooting" or why Margot Macomber shoots her husband.

Read till your eyeballs beg for mercy. And read a variety of things. We start by reading at least five papers a day—two locals and three nationals (*USA Today, The New York Times, The Wall Street Journal*). We'd tell you how much time we spend on the web each day, but then our wives and bosses would find out.

Research your favorite areas of interest. Curious as to what other critics thought about what really happened in Poe's "Ligeia," we did the necessary background research, only to discover we disagreed with previous critics and therefore had to come up with a better explanation. Likewise, convinced the critics didn't know why Duke Ferrara's last duchess died, we crafted a unique interpretation.

Communicate with colleagues. One day as we were heading to McDonald's for lunch, we were discussing the odd behavior of the narrator of Poe's "Berenice" and why he pulls the teeth of his departed lady. One of us joked that she was probably a vampire, and without her "fangs" she couldn't rise from the dead to bite him. Bingo, another publication. Another time we had a colleague in the next office publish a book about how so many of Browning's poems begin and end the same way. At that moment we were getting ready to teach *Hedda Gabler*, and we spotted the same artistic device in Ibsen's play.

Eavesdrop. Sitting at McDonald's and inhaling our super-sized French fries and Coke, we overheard a couple in the next booth discussing how the guy's sister had been bitten in church by a rattlesnake she was "handling." The result was not one, but two entirely different short stories.

Reflect on personal experience. Being egotists, we once figured out that we had spent a lot of our youth watching the boob tube, so our generation must have also. That insight led us to research television watching habits and resulted in one published article and seven scripts for educational television.

Keep notes. Sometimes when we are in the midst of a scholarly pregnancy, we don't have the time or energy to devote to orphan ideas that come to us. We jot them down on sheets of paper and toss them into a folder. In dry periods we adopt them and raise them to maturity. A note from the 1970's about the chronology of *The Scarlet Letter* lay dormant until it appeared in an article with our byline in the twenty-first century. We also photocopy items, gather pictures, and tear pages out of doctor-office magazines for keep for our muse. The margins of our classroom texts are dog-tracked with our blue ink.

Pay attention to media. We created a successful writing casebook for first-year students based on our all-time favorite rock song, Don McLean's "American Pie." Our constant use of popular culture references to *American Idol* and *Top Gun* led us to write two separate pedagogical pieces on using pop references to create a bridge between the student's and the literary world.

Adapt familiar concepts to new material. While we were never ones to milk our dissertations, we have utilized content knowledge gained in the writing of our treatises. One way we had made it through grad school in English was being able to apply our philosophy coursework to assignments and write a formulaic paper at the last minute on "An Existential Interpretation of ... " before the proverbial hat dropped or the sun also rose the next day. Thirty years later when we were stumped as to why so many doors appeared in Hemingway's "The Killers," we remembered the ur-grad student paper, and we had another publication. Charlie's dissertation involved Bernard Malamud's use of the grail myth. That literary motif provided the framework for a children's musical, "The Royal Easter Egg Riddle," an analysis of "Shiloh," and a deconstruction of Cheever's "The Swimmer."

Ideas abound everywhere. Once to prove that very point we opened the dictionary and with our eyes closed we each pointed to a word. "Innocent" and "pudding" became The Innocent Pudding, a rock band from the 60's that disappeared, and we had to write a short story to find out why.

Hal Blythe
Charlie Sweet
Eastern Kentucky University

_____

Performing Market Analysis: A Worthwhile Alternative

Most scholars, especially those fresh out of graduate school, have a familiar methodology for getting published. They write the article, often milking their own dissertation (though, as Seinfeld would say, not that there's anything wrong with that), then send it off to a journal in their field. An alternative approach to getting your scholarship published exists, one that we have found to be more effective.

In our early career as fiction writers, we were trying to break into the mystery market ... with little luck. We received rejections on the first 24 stories we submitted to *Ellery Queen's Mystery Magazine* (EQMM) accompanied by the dreaded rejection slip with the words: SORRY, BUT IT DOES NOT MEET OUR NEEDS. After a while we were convinced that a monkey was opening our envelopes, immediately stuffing our package in the enclosed return, and adding our favorite note.

Rather than continue the same write 'em-then-market-'em approach, we decided to take a different tact. As Poe scholars, we were quite familiar with his literary satire "How to Write a Blackwood Article." In this tale Poe suggests how to get published in a magazine to which William Blackwood gave his name. In essence, the story is what we call today market research.

In short, we're suggesting scholars think like the business world. Before McDonald's erects their golden arches on a street corner, they study the market—the local population, its demographics, traffic flow, etc. They want some hard evidence that their enterprise at this locale has an excellent chance of success. Market research, then, is an alternative route for creative writers and scholars to take to publication. Analyzing the particular market reveals tendencies and ups the odds for your seeing print.

So how does one go about researching the market?

Back in 1978 B.I. (Before the Internet), we performed market research by reading one year's worth of stories in *Ellery Queen's Mystery Magazine.* We made up a chart for each piece of fiction, noting its length, type of story, point of view, characters' characteristics, plot elements, setting, and even conclusion. We then crunched the numbers on 100-plus stories to reveal EQMM's tendencies. Afterwards, we crafted a story that faithfully followed those tendencies.

"Sudden Death," our 25th submission to EQMM, sold.

Basically, as scholars we did the same thing. We got hold of journals for which we thought we would like to write. Most had a general style sheet and publishing information in them. As we were writing and publishing short stories, one publication stood out, *Studies in Short Fiction* (SSF), so we subscribed to it and read every issue cover to cover the way we had the comic books of our youth. Unlike our passive reading of those four-color fantasies of yesteryear, we actually studied how the SSF articles were written. In those days new criticism was the dominant form of literary criticism, and after a while we mastered its tendencies, its approach, and even its vocabulary (why hadn't we been taught this kind of close reading in graduate school?). Over the years we published quite a few articles in SSF on Poe, Hemingway, Mason, and others. Of course, SSF wasn't the only journal we subjected to market analysis, and consequently it wasn't the only journal in which we published.

When we started out, it was also possible to write to various popular magazines for their "Tip Sheets," always enclosing an S.A.S.E. Now, with the Internet available, it's easier and quicker to locate the tips online; tendencies still reveal themselves through study, but with so many journals now online and available through the campus library, one no longer has to subscribe to them.

Other research can provide you insight into getting published. The Internet offers related help, especially with journal editors. Sometimes you can look up a specific journal and see the requirements for submission and to whom. Other times you can locate excellent insights into writing for publication in general. For instance, the 28 September 2007 issue of the *Chronicle of Higher Education* contains an excellent piece by Jeffrey Williams, editor of the *Minnesota Review,* who lists "several tendencies in academic writing to avoid": glossomania (excessive citation), indirection (being excessively roundabout), false difficulty, self-indulgence, and lazy language (e.g., "in other words"). He also points out that experienced scholars are easier to deal with than younger scholars because the former are more open to change (3-9). Moreover, both popular writers and scholars have blogs on subjects from culinary to crossword puzzle-solving tips.

Conferences are another excellent source of insight into publishing. Most major discipline conferences have panel discussions on publishing with notable journal editors on the panel. Some, like our Modern Language Association (MLA), get written up. And don't forget personal contact. Two years ago at the Lilly Conference on College Teaching we participated in a session on the scholarship of teaching and learning led by Greg Wentzell, editor of the *Journal on Excellence in College Teaching*. His active learning segment consisted of the audience acting as reviewers for the journal to assess manuscripts (and he was actually looking for journal reviewers). Afterwards, we struck up a conversation with him on what specific subjects he needed. A year later we had coffee with Greg, and he told us Miami University was starting a new publication right up our alley, *The Learning Communities Journal*. Guess what article we're working on right now?

Hal Blythe
Charlie Sweet
Eastern Kentucky University

The Most Important Writing Tool

Twenty acres, a tractor, and a toolbox, that's all we had and all we needed. When the old John Deere broke down, we just grabbed the toolbox and put it right. Writing's no different. Just keep a few tools...and know how to use them.

I keep a dictionary in my toolbox, but that's because I'm such a poor speller. I don't trust my computer speller because it doesn't always know which word I'm trying to spell. But I'm sure you are a better speller, so let's skip over the dictionary and go straight to my most important tool, the journal. That's right; the journal itself is my most important writing tool. I use it like a carpenter uses a blueprint.   As a couple of my friends like to say, "It works for me."

Here's how to use it. First, know what you want to achieve, both professionally and personally. Then pick out a couple of journals that match these goals. For example, if one of your goals is to earn tenure, choose a national or international refereed journal. If you are in a hurry to get published, choose a journal with an acceptance rate of at least 25 percent. What's that? How do you know the acceptance rate? That's easy. See one my June issue *Kappan* articles. If your journal isn't included, check Cabell's directories of publishing opportunities or just call the editor's office and ask for the acceptance rate. Next, choose a second journal published for the same audience, and preferably one with the same citation style (APA, Chicago, etc.)   Read every article in each issue. This is never done any more and it could ruin your reputation, but it won't kill you.

The most important thing to look for is a section titled *Author's Guidelines* or *Suggestions to Authors*. Here, the editors answer questions that we don't even know to ask. It's the mother lode. When you find it, put one finger on each sentence and leave it there until you have done what the editor told you to do. No, you're right; it isn't nuclear science, but I've written several physics grants and all of them were funded. I'm 99.9 percent sure that it helps to follow the rules and do it right.

While I'm trying to remember the second most important journal section to look for, think about the people who read this journal. A quarter-century of research tells me that the most common mistake that leads to rejection is failure to know the journal and its readers.

Now I remember the second most important thing; it's about themes. I've just surveyed 40 journals, and about half of all the articles in these journals last year related to a theme; so there are plenty of themes to choose from. But, you ask, why themes? You see, on average, editors receive only one-third as many manuscripts for themed issues. My background as a math teacher tells me that this means that simply by writing to a theme you can increase your acceptance rate by over 300 percent. That payoff isn't half bad, for doing nothing.

Now I recognize you. You are the one who attends my writing workshops and tries to find an exception to each of my suggestions. Right now, your mind is thinking, "We are told to write what we know and care about. What if there are no themes on my topic?" It's simple; align your topic with a theme. The principle is the same as with grant writing. I wanted money to create a performance-based teacher education program and none was available. But I found a request for proposals to address teacher burnout. So, I created a performance-based program that addressed teacher burnout. It was funded for a half-million dollars.

Now let's look for a journal section titled *Call for Manuscripts*. This publishing business is a buyer's market. On average, these editors receive five times as many manuscripts as they have space to use; some reject 19 out of every 20. But when you see a *Call for Manuscripts* section, this means the odds are reversed. They actually <u>need</u> your manuscript. So help them out. Now, make your manuscript look and sound like the articles in this journal. Make it about the same length as those articles. If your journal's articles have sub-headings, tables, charts, and references, make sure yours does, too. I believe that when you make your manuscript read so much like the articles in the journal that the editor and reviewers forget they are reading a manuscript, that's when you get accepted. Good luck!

Ken Henson
The Citadel

_____

2. Writing

Avoiding Writer's Block

One of the biggest problems we encounter in working with young (and sometimes not so young) creative writers is the infamous writer's block. Time and time again our students come to us with stories NOT in hand to lament that "I just went blank, and the longer I looked at the screen, the worse it got." We offer them a solution to their stasis that we've found works equally well for those who encounter a block when writing scholarship.

For years Hal's wife has cooked a mid-week dinner for members of their church to allow families to eat a nourishing meal and still participate in various church activities that evening. Serving over 100 people, Marsha and her crew couldn't possibly cook all the food at once even with all the ovens and burners available. To accomplish their task, they prepare the meal in stages. At any one time during the process, some of the food is being put together, some kept warm on heating trays, some cooking, and some being served.

Marsha's recipe can work for you as you "prepare" your scholarly articles. What we suggest is that you have more than one project underway at any given time—and we like to have pieces at various stages of their development. This week, for instance, we put the finishing touches on an article on assessment (and sent it to our editor), worked on a revision of a piece on organizing your class we're doing for a faculty development journal, and wrote a first draft for this tip. Having three projects at once keeps us fresh. If we feel our energy flagging on one article, we switch to another for a bit.

Multi-taskers are us.

With our assessment article in the email, we spent some time today doing our foundation research for a piece on revision we'll start writing tomorrow. For us, staging projects not only helps us avoid writer's block, but also lets us serve up a satisfying scholarly plate.

Hal Blythe
Charlie Sweet
Eastern Kentucky University

———————————————

Last In, First Out: Using Recent Scholarship

Long ago we cured our students of a particularly inefficient way of doing research in our discipline. Deciding to work on Poe or Hawthorne, our erstwhile American Literature scholars would produce a tentative bibliography filled with scholarship drawn from past decades, some seemingly reaching back to the dawn of America itself. When we questioned them about their sources, they claimed that those listed were first on their Google or EBSCO Host search or, rarely, books on the library's shelves. Unfortunately, we've discovered some new faculty members we've mentored fall prey to the same error in methodology—and they should know better.

While loading a bibliography with the most noted figures in the field can be impressive, starting your research with these findings might not be the best strategy. Nonetheless, we've found both students and colleagues unaware of what seems obvious: **begin your research with the most current pieces of scholarship.**

The last-in, first-out approach offers several advantages. One of the features we love about the APA documentation style (MLA is standard in our discipline) is that the form lists the date of the publication immediately following the author's name in the body of the article (in MLA the date doesn't appear until the Works Cited at the end). A quick glance at the text or the bibliography in APA allows a reader to sense just how current the scholarship is, how up-to-date the research used. Regardless of documentation, however, beginning with the most current research on your subject will allow you to include recent dates in your bibliography to give readers (and they do peruse those bibs) a first sense of your research's currency.

More importantly, **beginning with the most current research on your topic provides a shortcut in your research.** A writer appearing in a recent issue of a reputable journal will doubtless have done his/her due diligence (and peer reviewers will insist upon it), thus saving you hours of research. All (or least most) of the relevant research on the topic will be referenced by this writer; a quick scan of the bibliography will take you to the scholarship for review. And, of course, you can double-check this research if you don't think the publishing journal vetted it well enough or if you think the writer's slant was too narrow to include your prevailing interest.

But, as they say on infomercials, there's more. Reading through the review of literature will give you the scholar's "take" on what predecessors have written on the subject, usually with both strengths and weaknesses (a caveat: since arts & humanities publications are opinion-based, you are less apt to find both). You'll have to be sure not to be prejudiced by the writer's observations, but the insight gained can still be valuable.

Of course, the recent article's conclusions provide you with the "last word" on the topic. This material not only supplies information, but can offer you a stepping off point for your piece as you build upon or refute the writer's conclusions. Many of our articles have resulted from our disagreement with a view held by a contemporary scholar, and, interestingly, our publishing of an opposed position has led to a healthy exchange through the mails and in some cases through subsequent articles in scholarly journals. For instance, we recently published a rebuttal of an article that had in turn rebutted a piece of ours written twenty-five years ago.

Last in, first out might not be very encouraging to industry's workforce, but it's a positive principle in scholarship.

Hal Blythe
Charlie Sweet
Eastern Kentucky University

Use "End Notes" to Organize Scholarship

Most scholars find writing references in the correct format laborious. I've discovered an easy but effective way to copy articles and to store references for scholarly purposes. "End Notes" is an electronic tool that automatically organizes references for the writer. The software also allows scholars the opportunity to highlight important sentences in each article. To use this tool most effectively, by creating a research question, search for the most recent ten articles, electronically capture the entire article, highlight the important points in bold or in color, then store the information digitally. This process allows you to build a tremendous reference library that is in alphabetical order. When you get ready to write a paper on the subject, all the materials are stored and organized on your computer for easy use.

To write a scholarly paper, simply reread all the highlighted sentences in the electronic library, put these ideas in some kind of logical order, and create a topical outline. While all this research is fresh on your mind, begin to write a topical sentence for each paragraph and include the reference, e.g., Smith (2008). Next write one good paragraph at a time—just get the words on the page; then go back and rewrite the entire paper at least ten times. Even the most seasoned writers must rewrite. When the time comes, the cited references used in the paper will automatically be available for you to cut and paste from your electronic library. The reference page becomes the easiest part of the paper.

You might be interested to know that at the click of the button the "End Notes" software will change from APA style to MLA or Chicago. It will convert to the style you need for any audience. Scholarship just became a lot easier for people who detest typing references, have a difficult time organizing, and for those who must read and reread articles.

William L. Phillips
Eastern Kentucky University

Don't Use a Scalpel to Peel an Apple

One of my favorite people was the legendary football coach, Paul "Bear" Bryant. One event stands out. Coach Bryant had won more games than had any other coach, and his institution, The University of Alabama, had won more national championships than any other institution. A rookie player had made a great touchdown and had let everyone know it by spiking the ball. The Bear calmly called him over to the bench and said, "Son, don't act like this is the only time you have ever made a great play."

I liked the Bear because he had class. He saw beyond the play. He even saw beyond the game. He never signed a player before talking to the player's mother. He let her know that to him playing ball was secondary; his main goal was to have her son earn a college degree. And like another great coach with class, Joe Paterno, the Bear used his own money to provide academic scholarships for his players.

When I evaluate manuscripts, I think about that kid who celebrated his success by showing off. The majority of the manuscripts I read have this kid's name all over them. Every big, fancy word and every paragraph-long sentence filled with jargon says, "Look at me. I am a scholar. I have my terminal degree!" Where did we ever learn to equate erudite, pompous writing with scholarship? Jargon isn't necessarily bad. When needed, it is an important tool, like a scalpel is to a brain surgeon. But in the manuscripts I evaluate, when I rake back the jargon, I don't see the great thoughts of a surgeon. In fact, I don't see much of anything.

Most editors are scholars, and real scholars will not be impressed with two-dollar words when 25-cent words will work better. When you write, forget the editor. Write directly to the readers as though you were trying to help them. Isn't that the purpose of writing? Can't you help them more by using simple, familiar words, short paragraphs, and crisp sentences?

Because I am approaching my word limit, let's make one quick return to the football field. One of my favorite quarterbacks was Jay Barker. Jay didn't have a particularly strong arm. In fact, many people criticized him, saying that he had a weak arm. Jay wasn't known for his complex strategies or his erudite game plans. In fact, Jay didn't seem to have any of those features that make a quarterback glow. The only thing Jay seemed to have going for him was a simple knack for winning. He held one of the best

---

winning records ever held at the school that had won the most national championships. When I receive journal manuscripts to evaluate, I always hope to find at least one written by a Jay Barker, who, without boast or brag, just quietly gets the job done.

My assignment was to give a tip. So, here's my tip. Don't write until you have something worth saying. Then, say it simply and clearly, and stop.

Ken Henson
The Citadel

How to Create a Poster Presentation Using PowerPoint

Broadening the traditional view of scholarship, Boyer (1990) identifies four key dimensions of scholarly activity for college and university professors: teaching, discovery, integration and application. While encouraging acceptance of a wide range of scholarly endeavors, Boyer also highlights that "some dimensions of scholarship are universal- mandates that apply to all" (1990, pg. 27). One of these universal dimensions of scholarship is the need for peer validation of the value and contribution of one's work. As explained by Boyer, "The work of the professoriate- regardless of the form it takes-must be carefully assessed. Excellence is the yardstick by which all scholarship must be measured... Faculty who engage in research, in teaching, in service, or in integrative work must demonstrate to the satisfaction of peers that high performance standards have been met." (1990, pg. 28). As indicated by this standard, scholarship requires that faculty communicate and validate their work within the larger professional community. For professional activities to be recognized as scholarship, they must be publicly disclosed, open to critique and evaluation, and communicated in a format that allows others to build on the knowledge.

While there are countless ways for faculty members to disseminate their research, conference presentations provide one of the most popular means of sharing one's work in a scholarly environment. Specifically, many faculty members elect to present their intellectual work in poster format at professional conferences as it provides an informal public forum for discussing, validating and extending one's work. In contrast to the formal oral presentation which consists of one-way communication, poster presentations allow for ongoing dialogue between the researcher and interested peers.

In our experience as faculty developers, we find that faculty are eager to present their scholarly work in a poster format at professional conferences, yet many lack the technical skills to create their poster in the single sheet format that is popular at today's conferences. To address this barrier in the dissemination of research, we created an online, multimedia presentation to teach faculty how to utilize basic PowerPoint software to create a professional poster presentation. The purpose of our 'tip' is to share this online, open access resource with all faculty to aid in their own professional enhancement for presentation preparation using tools they already have at their disposal. While virtually all faculty are familiar with PowerPoint software, many have limited its use to creating classroom-based, lecture presentations. The online, multimedia presentation provides an audio-narrated, step-by-step demonstration showing faculty how to utilize basic PowerPoint functions to create a professional poster that can then be printed on a large-format plotter. The presentation is self-paced and can be easily accessed online at: http://www.park.edu/cetl/quicktips/CreatingaPoster.html; the online availability provides an on-demand resource for faculty to utilize while creating their poster presentations and is user friendly for the novice or veteran faculty member.

In the first six months that the multimedia presentation was available online, hit counter records indicate that it was viewed by over 350 professionals. The value of this resource has been reinforced in the unsolicited qualitative feedback we've received; as expressed via email by one faculty member: "Wow! What a great resource! I just learned to make my first 'real' poster presentation. Not only am I ready for the XXX conference, but I am now planning to teach my students how to share their findings in a poster format. Thank you!" It is our hope, that in sharing this resource, we can offer all professionals the opportunity to create a professional presentation through which they can be proud to disseminate their scholarly work.

B. Jean Mandernach
Emily Donnelli-Sallee
Amber Dailey-Hebert
Park University

Nothing Is Written—Everything Is Rewritten

Headed for an appointment he's not sure he wants to keep, T. S. Eliot's famous man about town, J. Alfred Prufrock, claims, "There will be time to murder and create ... /And time yet for a hundred visions and revisions ...." While we hope that you don't dread an appointment with the editor of your favorite journal, we do have a few comments about revision you might find helpful.

If writing a draft of a scholarly piece is difficult, rewriting seems next to impossible. But it can be a valuable experience if you can get past certain negative attitudes.

Good writers never rewrite. Though he never claimed to be a scholar, Ernest

Hemingway admitted in a letter to a friend that he had to rewrite the ending to *A Farewell to Arms* over forty times. And while we can't claim Papa Hemingway's status, we'll tell you that a recently published article of ours went through a dozen or so versions before an editor ended our misery. Hey, even Moses had to go back up the mountain for a rewriting of those Commandments—and their author is usually held in pretty high regard.

All my words are sacred. We won't refer again to the guy Charlton Heston made famous, but we will say that William Faulkner (yes, he did flunk freshman comp at the University of Mississippi, but went on to a fairly successful career) once claimed that writers must learn to "Kill your darlings," and that famous Frenchman Gustave Flaubert edited his first novel manuscript by tossing it in the fireplace. Seriously, writing is like carpentry: first, you put up the basic structure, then come back for the finish work. Think of your first draft of an article as the frame and be willing in the spirit of *Flip This House* to rearrange, recolor, and even replace individual details in order to achieve the desired overall effect.

Rewriting is a Herculean task. As Isaac Bashevis Singer puts it, "Experience has shown me that there are no miracles in writing. The only thing that produces good writing is hard work" (please excuse all these religious allusions, but writing is somewhat spiritual, right?). Look on the positive side. When you revise, you work with something already written down. In the first draft ideas had to be translated into words—now your task is simply to scrutinize the words to produce maximum effectiveness. Rather than having to create ex nihilo (whoops, we've done it again), you have some clay with which to work.

All negatives aside, revision affords you a chance to reconsider your ideas in light of time, additional evidence, and perhaps even the studied opinions of colleagues and peer-reviewers. In fact, we would suggest you never proofread alone; our rule of thumb is that it takes six eyes to proof any work; another rule is that no matter how long and how many eyes proof, some errors will be missed.

Sure, lots of time can be involved, and learning to purge some of those golden words and phrases can be painful, but a willingness to revise can make that appointment with the editor a much more pleasurable experience.

Hal Blythe
Charlie Sweet
Eastern Kentucky University

_____

3. Submission

The Staircase Approach to Becoming A Published Scholar

These days when instructors can tape their students' in-class writing to the wall or post it on a Blackboard website and call it "published," the notion of becoming a published writer is cheapened. If by "publishing" you mean getting your scholarship into a peer-reviewed journal, then we have a simple methodology you can try.

An important caveat: don't write yourself a piece of scholarship and then just email it off with a wish and a prayer. Your chances for publication will improve if you do two things—market research (see our companion piece) and climbing the staircase of scholarship.

1. **Begin locally.** All scholarship is an attempt for you to join in a larger conversation, so start at your university. Almost every piece of scholarship we've published began with something we tried in class, usually but not always in a graduate class. We know that grad students probably aren't experts enough to know what you're discussing with them, but they can tell you when you seem way off base. Maybe you simply show a first draft to that colleague across the hall who is in your area. 600 published works ago we were three offices apart and talked over an idea for ITV over tennis. Just recently we tried out the first draft of an article on building a strategic plan, a subject not smack in our domain, on a colleague who heads the University's Division of Institutional Research. In another case, we started a cross-disciplinary faculty learning community on scholarly writing, and when it was time for us to have our writing critiqued, we submitted a piece on the concept of faculty learning communities. One of the group turned out to be an expert in statistics, definitely an area of weakness for us, so we asked him to join us. And since the article dealt with educational research, we asked the dean of the College of Education if he also wanted to be a co-author. A few years ago an article that we ended up publishing in *The Teaching Professor* had its debut as a presentation at our campus Teaching & Learning Center.

2. **Present at state or regional conferences.** Our department is part of a state-wide organization that rotates its annual March meetings around the Commonwealth. One of our early publications was at just such a meeting. Another time we did a presentation at the national convention of the Popular Culture Association because it was held just a two-hour drive away in Louisville. Two years into our collabo-writing we helped a colleague organize a meeting of the International Conference on Linguistics in Richmond; in return, he helped us to get on the program and to prepare a suitable paper. This year

Kentucky's Council on Postsecondary Education is holding a conference 25 miles away in Lexington, and we're trying out an idea there, and after the presentation we're hoping to enlist the aid of faculty developers at other regional campuses in co-writing with us so that our idea can be utilized as part of a state-wide survey of campuses. The best part of presentation at local and regional conferences is the question and answer session afterward and even meeting with some interested parties for drinks and dinner. We once got into a running two-day conversation at the Lilly Conference on College Teaching in Miami, Ohio, that resulted in a publication.

3. **Go to national conventions with your paper.** When we were getting started, we had what we considered a novel take on a short story by Edgar Allan Poe, so we submitted a proposal to the International Conference on the Fantastic (it helped that the group was meeting in south Florida during February). At the convention we ran into some big guns in Poe scholarship, and they were quite generous with their times. We ended up with quite a few publications on Poe and even an invitation to address the annual meeting of the Poe Society. At a national meeting of the Popular Culture Association in St. Louis we attended a session on western films and met Mike Nevins, a law professor at a local university and a frequent contributor to *Ellery Queen's Mystery Magazine.* Since we were also breaking into the mystery field, we tapped Mike's expertise then and for a long time afterwards. Perhaps our most important contact came at the first annual meeting to honor John D. MacDonald. We ended up with a presentation ("Ask Mr. Mystery"); a contact with the conference organizer, Ed Hirshberg, who would start inviting us to the Florida Suncoast Writers Conference; and, most importantly, a meeting with John D. himself, who opened many doors in publishing and into the locked room of how to write a good mystery. Last year at the Lilly Conference we were chatting with Greg Wentzell, the editor for the *Journal of Excellence in College Teaching,* when he happened to mention that his university was getting ready to launch a new journal on faculty development, a current area of interest for us. What you have to say at these meetings is often less important than whom you meet.

4. **Write short notes before long articles.** Erskine Caldwell of *Tobacco Road* fame once wrote, "Publication of early work is what a writer needs most of all in life." Your biggest publication may not be your first, but your first, like your first love, is the one you are always going to remember. When Charlie first came to Eastern, the chair told him, "Your first year here I want you to concentrate on being the best teacher you possibly can"—we are a regional comprehensive university—"after that, I want to see at least one publication per year." Charlie figured it was going to be hard to break into *PMLA* or *American Literature* right out of grad school, so he took an idea he had first noticed in his Am Lit I class on Edward Arlington Robinson, wrote it up as a note, and submitted it to a small journal in Robinson's home state of Maine; the article was published in the *Colby Library Journal.* The first publication is like that first contact in a game of football; you play a lot better after it.

Baseball players in the June draft rarely jump directly to the major leagues. They keep on climbing a staircase that started years before in T-ball, Little League, and high school. We suggest that such a staircase approach might help you get to the Big Show in your field as well.

Hal Blythe
Charlie Sweet
Eastern Kentucky University

Short, but Effective

In sports size often matters—but sometimes in surprising ways. While standing 6' 8" often helps in basketball and weighing 400-plus pounds furthers chances for success in sumo wrestling, even average size can hinder one's chances in gymnastics, where apparatuses and mandatory routines put a premium on smaller stature.

So often we've seen experienced colleagues spend years working on that one great piece of scholarship that will assure them a hallowed place in their discipline ... and tenure. Certainly nothing is wrong or wasteful in devoting years to that *magnum opus*—if that project is completed. Unfortunately, putting all the publishing eggs in one basket can lead to frustration. In dealing with some of our younger colleagues in recent years, we noticed that their idea of scholarly endeavor called for a book or a major article right out of the gate. Realizing that for most of them that goal wasn't realistic (though it may be a little down the line as tenure gleams in the distance), we adopted an approach that had us mentoring them in the note or short research article as a way of "breaking into" the scholarly world.

A caveat: we know that some fields don't recognize the short article as important. On the other hand, the profession has come a long way since a former chair told us his way of measuring an article's significance: the greater the word count, the better the article.

For most, then, the note offers several advantages for the beginner. By focusing on a single aspect of a subject, the novice scholar is not apt to feel overwhelmed. The limited scope allows the writer to do a thorough job with the research and thus feel that his or her idea indeed makes a contribution to the scholarly conversation. In addition, the limited scope allows the writer to complete the project in a manageable amount of time. Rather than agonizing over the prospect of spending months or years before seeing results, the writer can take the piece from idea to submission in a short period of time.

Writing a short note is easier because it's less a chore to find short chunks of time to work on sections of it. We've read research over breakfast and added it to a note as soon as we got to the office. A working lunch becomes a habit. That half hour between the end of class and the start of the next committee meeting can be quite productive.

Furthermore, the note or short article can serve as a threshold to larger projects. A brief study of a small group concerning voting patterns, for instance, might lead to a more comprehensive investigation down the road. Years ago we wrote a note on John Cheever's use of a small image in his classic story "The Swimmer." That brief piece engendered 14 additional articles on the story and the basis for a book-length study. Analyzing a small subject intensely usually helps you spot other promising avenues.

It has been our experience that many journal editors are on the lookout for short—but strong—pieces of scholarship. In our discipline, English, most journals welcome notes and short articles to balance the many lengthy pieces they receive. And nothing pleases a new scholar more than "I am pleased to accept ...."

One last tip. We always tell our students to write on a subject so small they don't think there's enough for a scholarly piece. The challenge usually makes them dig deeper into the subject because they have a minimum word count to attain. The same challenge works for those on the tenure-track.

Hal Blythe
Charlie Sweet
Eastern Kentucky University

Scholarly Articles:
Two-Fers and Three-Fers

Question—when is a scholarly article not just a scholarly article? Answer—when it's two or three.

Most dissertations can be milked for two or three publications, but that's not what we're talking about. What we want you to do is think big; when you pick a topic on which to write, tell yourself you are going to get two or three publications out of it.

How can one multiply into three? Actually we have used a few approaches.

One, in general when you write a medium or longer piece of scholarship, you know you inevitably condense one part of your essay, sometimes for word count and some-times because you think it's a minor point. Save these pieces; allude to them in your longer work, and then develop that embryo into a separate note or longer piece. For instance, when we were writing on Cheever's "The Swimmer," we ran across two Shakespearian references. Rather than write an article, we wrote two notes; unfortu-nately, we were thwarted because our editor thought we ought to combine them, but that's another story.

Two, sometimes when you are treating an aspect in a work, something else jumps out at you. We have spent our scholarly career searching out patterns and motifs that inform literary works. When we were writing about the Grail myth in Mason's "Shiloh," we noticed some other patterns that eventually became topics for other published pieces.

Three, every argument has a counter-argument. In fact, one of our favorite writing exercises in first-year English involved the argument paper; for one assignment we would have our students argue one side of a local issue, and for their next paper they had to take the opposite point of view. We sometimes followed our own assignment in the scholarly arena. Once we wrote an article on Lardner's barber in "Haircut" being a dupe, and then we took the opposite side and argued he was the clever architect of a conspiracy. We look at lit from both sides now and then.

Fourth, the architect of a conspiracy theory struck us as an excellent slant, so we then applied the same idea to a story by Ernest Hemingway, "The Short, Happy Life of Francis Macomber." Another time we wrote about the narrator of Camus' "The Renegade" as a paranoid schizophrenic (the term was then in the DSM); years later we returned to that scene and demonstrated how Gilman's narrator of "The Yellow Wallpaper" suffers from the same condition.

Fourth, sometimes you can publish the same basic idea in two different markets, the scholarly journal and the popular magazine. Our work with instructional television (ITV), for instance, has led to parallel articles on audience in *College English* and *Writer's Digest*, while our interest in Poe's Dupin tales took us to *Poe Studies* and *Clues*.

Our moms were both thrifty women who taught their boys always to get the best value for their money—and their ideas.

Hal Blythe
Charlie Sweet
Eastern Kentucky University

_____

Beating Rejectionslipitis

Joseph Conrad, *The Heart of Darkness* guy, once read a review of his latest work over breakfast, and the subsequent grumbling didn't come from his stomach. When his wife asked him why he was so upset and didn't he want criticism, he replied tersely, "Hell, no! I want praise."

So do we all—even scholars. And while the Conrads of the world receive their praise in the form of huge royalty checks ... and Oscar statues, most often scholars gain acknowledgement of our accomplishments through publication in a book or journal, acceptance to present at a conference (leading, of course, to promotion, tenure, and the really big bucks), and a rare pat on the back from our colleagues/chair. Unfortunately, many times instead of praise, we get that dreaded printed slip in our SASE or email, resulting in a case of rejectionslipitis, a progressive disease that with each successive rejection renders its victims depressed, inert, and unable to return to either research or the computer.

Let the good doctors offer you a prescription to cure this debilitating malady.

Change your attitude toward that rejection. As we point out in "Files and Inventory," keeping a record of the disposition of your submitted piece is important, and we'll admit that early in our collaborative career some of our articles were rejected so many times we had to start new columns to record the bad news. And some of the criticism was pretty deflating. Once we submitted an article on Robert Browning's "My Last Duchess" to a respected (but stuffy) journal. Our article took a rather iconoclastic approach to Browning's masterpiece to which one reviewer scribbled, "With names like Blythe and Sweet, this article must be some kind of joke." Yes, we did get rejected, but the personal sting was impetus to send the piece to a more prestigious journal, where it was accepted. Those tales of Margaret Mitchell's *Gone With the Wind* being rejected by thirty-six publishers or Richard Hooker's seven-year, twenty-two publishers' trek to sell *M*A*S*H* are not unique to creative writers; rejection is just as much a fact of the scholarly life. But, take heart in knowing that your possession of a rejection means you have at least written something and somebody has read it. That effort alone puts you in select company.

Learn from the rejection. If the slip, letter, or email says something as simple as "This does not meet our current needs," the editor probably means just that. Rather than commenting on the quality of your work, the rejection might come because the journal is backlogged with accepted articles, it has recently accepted an article close to yours in content, or your article does not exactly fit the journal's requirements for length, slant, or style. See our "Performing Market Analysis" and Ken Henson's "The Most Important Writing Tool" for advice on researching journals in order to tailor your submissions to a particular publication.

Study the rejection carefully. A common practice in many fields is for editors to include their reviewers' comments with the rejection, most of which are infinitely more helpful than the one we received from the Browning journal. Recently we had an article appear in *Pedagogy* that was the result of a five-year process of revision. When we first submitted the piece to Journal A, it was rejected with a detailed list of weaknesses included. After a few minutes of despair and cursing, we set to addressing the issues, then resubmitted to Journal A. Again, we came up short. This time after revision we submitted it to Journal B (another journal in the field), got rejected, rewrote according to suggestions, resubmitted, and were rejected again. When we rewrote and resubmitted to journal A/*Pedagogy*, our five-year odyssey ended with publication. Remember, rejection doesn't close the door to you if you learn from the process, are willing to rewrite, and you persist.

Keep your manuscript circulating for a reasonable time. No article, regardless of quality, can be published if it sits in your computer or a cardboard box at the back of your closet. Every time your work makes a stop at an editor's desk, you have a chance to pick up valuable advice or even acceptance for publication. This month we had a story appear in a popular magazine, but the interesting thing is we wrote the first version of the story over 25 years ago and had it rejected. When we saw the popular magazine was looking for stories in a certain vein, we made some changes (including updates), resubmitted, and sold it. In the seventies we wrote an article on Hemingway that we loved but editors did not. A few years ago we were looking over our small collection of unpublished works, reread the article, saw immediately what was missing that our younger selves hadn't, did the necessary research, rewrote, and the result appeared in print.

Rejectionslipitis doesn't have to be fatal. When treated properly, in fact, it can result in a stronger, healthier body of scholarship.

Hal Blythe
Charlie Sweet
Eastern Kentucky University

Collaborative Scholarship

Mentoring the Publication Process

Faculty at primarily undergraduate teaching institutions often struggle to balance the demands of the classroom with expectations to engage in professional scholarship. Those individuals who have actively elected to position their careers in teaching-focused institutions likely focus their efforts and time on teaching, perhaps without engaging in extensive research or publishing that may be typical of research-based institutions. Many master teachers, who are actively engaged in strategies to enhance the effectiveness of teaching and learning within their classrooms, fail to share their expertise and experiences with a larger academic audience due to a lack of familiarity or experience with the process of scholarly publication. While research-oriented institutions often have an extensive peer network of experienced researchers to informally guide and facilitate the research process, resources to facilitate publishing one's scholarly work may be lacking at teaching-oriented schools.

To address this void at our own institution, we created a Faculty Scholarship Mentor Program sponsored by the Center for Excellence in Teaching and Learning. The Faculty Scholarship Mentor Program provides informal mentoring to faculty interested in pursuing independent scholarly activities. The goal of the program is to provide faculty with an informal sounding board from which they may develop, implement and disseminate their scholarly projects. Through informal, non-structured interactions, Faculty Scholarship Mentors:

1) help define and clarify project ideas,
2) provide guidance on university funding sources,
3) facilitate navigation of the Institutional Review Board,
4) provide ongoing feedback concerning project implementation,
5) read and critique project reports,
6) provide guidance on dissemination outlets, and
7) assist with the publication submission process.

While the mentor is not directly involved with the specific implementation, analysis or communication of the project, mentors provide the necessary support to allow faculty to pursue scholarly endeavors. As such, mentors work with interested faculty across all stages of research development. From guidance in the brainstorming and drafting stages of manuscript development, to assistance in finding an appropriate journal outlet, to understanding and responding to reviewers' concerns, the Faculty Scholarship Mentor simultaneously provides support and information to help guide the novice researcher through the publication process.

The Faculty Scholarship Mentor Program focuses on the process behind conducting and publishing research rather than the topic or methodologies of the specific research endeavor. While graduate programs typically provide extensive training on how to structure, implement and analyze research, they often do not adequately train faculty on how to navigate institutional policies concerning research (such as funding sources and IRB approvals) or how to navigate the publishing process (such as selecting an appropriate journal, writing a submission cover letter, responding to reviewers/editors, revising a manuscript for resubmission, etc). The explicit goal of the Faculty Scholarship Mentor program is to provide the necessary support and assistance to encourage faculty to publish their research in a relevant scholarly outlet.

The value of the Faculty Scholarship Mentor Program was expressed in an unsolicited email from one faculty who wrote: "Once again, we are in need of your assistance with something if you are willing. Because this is the first piece we have ever published, we do not know what comes next. What volume will the piece be in and what month will it come out? In other words, we really want to physically hold it in our hands...and celebrate while we pass it around and make/purchase copies for our friends and families! A very sincere thank you to you, XXX. I have to tell you that in all honesty, I didn't think I would ever publish anything. I believe I am a good teacher, but being academically productive in terms of publishing seemed an impossibility. My husband and I have 4 children under 8 years old, and life is busy balancing parenting and working. I didn't know when I would have time to sit down and actually write anything beyond field trip permission slips for our children and notes for classroom preparation for my classes. And I would have probably given up, were it not for your kind words early on in this process."

As a growing number of teaching institutions continue to adopt the Boyer model of scholarship and create new expectations for faculty to show evidence of their scholarly teaching, it is critical that resources and support are available to assist them in this journey. The Faculty Scholarship Mentor Program is one way we can all develop as academic professionals and learn how best to share our teaching excellence and lessons learned.

B. Jean Mandernach
Amber Dailey-Hebert
Emily Donnelli-Sallee
Park University

_____

Collaborative Research Works for Us

One method of scholarship that has worked well for us has been a collaborative research effort between an instructor and instructional designer. We have found that the instructor and the instructional designer share a common desire.... to provide pedagogically sound instruction. Therefore, both parties were motivated to engage in developing the course as well as collect data on the effectiveness of the instructional components offered through the course. In the process of developing instruction, we collaborated on the development of research questions on the methodology of the instruction and on the effectiveness of the instruction applied to the course content.

For a graduate-level Introduction to Counseling course, Kim, the instructor, and Paula, the instructional designer, worked together to develop the course and the course content over a period of 5 months. Through this type of collaborative effort, innovative instructional products or techniques were offered and piloted within the course. After the course and/or the instructional components of a course were developed, we worked together to conduct a research study to gather information about the effectiveness of the course and the instructional products provided.

The information gathered in this effort was then analyzed from the differing perspectives of the instructor (the content expert) and the instructional designer (the pedagogy expert). This dual perspective then allowed us to challenge each other's perspectives and to strengthen the data analysis that each produced. A side benefit of this form of collaboration from different perspectives is that the results can be interpreted and then reported in different professional arenas. Our collaboration has generated presentations and articles in both counselor education venues and instructional design venues.

We believe that when educators work collaboratively to engage in the kinds of activities that research promotes, they begin to value research as a process. The process of research can be expedited when both researchers have direct access to the course materials and methodologies as well as the course statistics on student usage. A great deal of what is perceived by the student versus what is "real" can be explored as the researchers (the instructor and instructional designer) work together to explore instructional methods and/or products and receive student feedback on their uses.

This research method was effective for this specific course, but could also be used for any course where new or innovative instructional strategies and/or technologies are tied to content specific material or where one set of instructional strategies or technologies used could be compared to another. For example, once the data is collected in one specific course, the data collection methods can be utilized in a longitudinal study (collecting data in the same course offered in later terms) or through a comparative study by collecting, summarizing and comparing data in a different course entirely or in a similar course using a different instructional design. Either way, rich data are generated that allow comparisons and/or summative data. We have found that a shared research experience can promote collegiality and experimentation that help to develop better instructional opportunities for students as well as rich scholarship opportunities for faculty and staff through publications and presentations.

Kim Naugle
Paula Jones
Eastern Kentucky University

Professional Learning Communities: A New Approach to Scholarship

In our primary role of faculty developers, we have lately grown disenchanted with the traditional presentation method of development and commensurately elated about the possibilities of an alternative method, the professional learning community (PLC). Although John Dewey proposed learning communities in the early twentieth century and foreign developers regularly employ them, American higher education has been slow to utilize their potential.

What is a professional learning community? Basically a PLC consists of several traits:

- Usually cross-disciplinary (often combining faculty and professional staff)
- 8-12 members or less (the literature often suggests even 15, but we have found that too many participants and thus not effective) plus two facilitators (the literature usually suggests one but for practical and pedagogical reason we prefer a duo)
- Active, collaborative learning experience
- Regularly structured scholarly activities (with a scholarly text as the focus)
- Semester-length (though the literature suggests letting them run a year)
- Payment of a stipend plus allowance for food and resources
- Creation of an end product (e.g., scholarship, conference presentation, syllabus revision, or teaching experience).

Each PLC costs us about $8,000, and this semester we are running ten of them, even asking other units to share the cost. Three of our PLCs not only use scholarship as part of the methodology, but for them scholarship is the subject.

The first, the Maki Book Group, we formed around the notion of writing a chapter of a book for noted assessment guru, Peggy Maki. Peggy has visited our campus in previous years to run workshops on assessment, and we have kept in touch. When she

Shared Tips for the Classroom   45

told us that Stylus was interested in her doing a book containing case studies on successful campus-wide assessment strategies, we volunteered to do a chapter. We put out a call to the campus and brought seven others into the community, including two from the office of Institutional Research, the General Education Coordinator, and the Dean of University programs. We acted as co-facilitators for a project that has actually stretched out over two semesters, and just last week we sent off a 6,000-word chapter to Peggy for her assessment. While she's the final arbiter of how well we did what she asked, we feel we learned a lot about the writing process and even more about how scholarship is performed outside our discipline.

The other two PLCs on scholarship were created by partnering with the College of Education (COE). We kicked off these two communities early last semester by cohosting a day-long workshop on scholarly writing and brought in an outside expert, Ken Henson. At the workshop we informed the participants that as a follow-up to the theoretical knowledge they had learned we would be running a PLC. When we had twice as many faculty sign up as we had anticipated, we broke them into two communities. We agreed to facilitate Writing Group I, but our methodology was different from the Maki group. We decided not to work on a common article, but basically to go round-robin and help each other with scholarship. Always willing to experiment, we also decided not to use a common text. When we started discussing what we wished to write, two members of the group shared a common interest with our subject, and so we agreed to cowrite with them. We grew so enamored with our research that we decided to present it also at a state-wide conference.

Regardless of the exact form, the PLC seems a very productive way to generate scholarship. Next semester we may try some more variations.

Hal Blythe
Charlie Sweet
Eastern Kentucky University

The Effects of Caffeine on Creativity

Ever have a mental block when it comes to scholarship? Facing a blank page can be quite frustrating. We've faced the same blank computer screen and have suffered through some publication dry spells. The temporary inability to focus on one idea long enough to thoroughly research and write about it, or not have the ability to come up with an idea to begin with, can be frustrating when you enjoy and/or are required to be active in the creative and scholarly arena. Long-term droughts of ideas can seem disastrous. A group of colleagues from diverse academic arenas at EKU recently stumbled upon a secret that has stirred up the creative juices and has gotten a pot full of ideas brewing. Our secret, we believe, is caffeine!

The previous book in the "It Works" series thoroughly addressed various tips and viewpoints that make clear the many benefits of working collaboratively. We whole-heartedly agree, and thus, we meet on a regular basis for coffee and creative inspiration.

If you think about it, this idea of sharing intellectual conversation over coffee and its power for stimulating large doses of energy should not be surprising. Take note at your next faculty meeting. Better yet, pay attention to what transpires between your profes-sional peers before and after your next professional conference/convention meeting when you are in the presence of peers whom you might only see once or twice annually. You know what happens. We become our students. We are excited to see each other. We cannot stop talking. Ideas and conversations flow with ease. If only we could bottle that creative energy that occurs when we gather with like-minds. Kindred spirits seem to allow for the flow of ideas and thoughts that otherwise seem to be lost in the world of everyday academia.

Admittedly, not all groupings of colleagues will result in the perfect blend. Not all have kindred spirits or common interests, which could hinder creative thoughts. We all bring unique strengths into such an arranged partnership, and it is possible that those involved could be so similar that the group can never seem to get beyond the stage of brainstorming for ideas. There is strength in numbers, as the saying goes, and that is what has helped us "caffeine friends" to find each other and become writing colleagues. Actu-ally, more than colleagues we have become coffee buddies who enjoy exploring ideas, creating projects, thinking about how to package what we love and share it with others. Our mentors at Eastern Kentucky University are Hal Blythe and Charlie Sweet, who have been writing friends, colleagues, and collaborators on over 600 written pieces. What a model from which to learn.

During coffee and conversation we never have trouble finding commonalities in our various fields or areas of expertise. We take notes, we discuss, we dream about new projects, we collaborate, we also help each other to stay focused--and we drink coffee! Frequently, when our cups are foaming over with too many distracting ideas (you could call this our "percolating" phase), we make a point to take notes for later when the ideas might be used in future articles or projects. It should be noted that the "extra" ideas that get stirred up are often the ones that turn into the most exciting ideas for researching or writing.

Knowing your partners is the sugar that is added to the coffee. You might say it is the sweetest part of these caffeinated conversations. The professional friendships that are formed with colleagues, knowing that they understand you as a friend, as a colleague, as a writer, as a dreamer, and knowing each other's intellect, strengths and weaknesses make this the sweetest and most precious part of this special blend. From the partner-ship comes learning about each other's families, exploring what makes each of us tick, attending to our desires to write and to become experts in our different fields. We also achieve a greater understanding and appreciation for those outside our specific content areas. Few of our friends outside of academia understand the drive to teach and learn from one another, nor the desire that we feel to publish and to tell others what we have learned from our partnership.

Searching for what works best for everyone has been a crucial ingredient when trying to find the right mix. Whether deciding who will be the note taker for the session, arranging the dates for our meetings, or who starts the article, we find that the mix has to be just right for us to be productive. We find face-to-face meetings are helpful in such an arrangement. The difficulty comes in finding a time that works for all involved and setting aside time for caffeine-filled creative meetings of the minds. We meet every Thursday from 8:00 – 9:30 at the campus coffee house. This time is sacred. We have to continually work on finding balance, the proper mix, to make sure that we place a priority on this time and not let other demands get in the way.

Of course electronic communications are priceless when it comes to keeping the creative momentum percolating, addressing the details, answering questions that were generated over coffee, or posing new questions and ideas after all have had some time to brew. Being able to zip off in an e-mail a new thought, a book title, an article, or something new we have seen keeps us in constant contact with our coffee friends. These electronic communications are the various flavors that we add to our coffee. The blends are constantly changing, with each of us adding our individual flavor. We find that many times once we have tried a new flavor, whether it is a new writing style, a new idea or a unique project, the result is that our group grows richer.

The effects of caffeine on us have changed our views on scholarship, but also our hopes, our dreams and our inspirations about sharing our love of not only coffee but the writing partnership we have formed. We have all the ingredients in place for a wonderful cup of coffee brimming over with just the right mix of flavor, sugar, and cream. We all recommend the effects of caffeine on creativity. It has been the best darn cup of coffee for brewing up creative ideas until they are overflowing.

Delinda Lybrand
Julie Alsip Bucknam
Gay Sweely
MaryAnn Kolloff
Eastern Kentucky University

_____

Encouraging Community-Based Scholarship

The WKU Alive Center for Community Partnerships (CCP) is committed to addressing a wide variety of regional needs through collaboration between community members and university faculty, staff, and students. A vital component of our overall strategy is the application of *community-based* scholarship. In essence, our aim is to meet practical needs in such a way that results in high quality research and student learning.

The guiding principles of these community-based projects are based on the collaborative nature of the work. This collaboration is intended to span the whole of the project, from the planning to the presentation stages. We are quick to recognize that there are multiple levels of expertise in play in any such effort – both in the community and in the academic department.

In order to support these activities, we have instituted an *Engaged Department Grant* program that encourages academic departments to pursue community-based scholarship. The typical process is as follows:

- The CCP maintains a database of identified community needs and continually communicates these to university faculty.
- Interested faculty, with the support of his or her department, will work with the community partner and a CCP staff member to design a project addressing the recognized need. Then the faculty member will apply for an Engaged Department Grant that allows for teaching release time and/or funding for project expenses.
- The CCP serves as a vital link between the university and community partner throughout the process. The aim is to maintain open communication, provide support, and encourage student participation in the project through service-learning experiences.
- A staff member of the CCP provides guidance and resources allowing for the generation of scholarship based on the experience. Such outlets include publication, conference presentation, and local presentation to the impacted population.

Faculty members who demonstrate an exceptional commitment toward community-based research and teaching have the opportunity to be appointed as a CCP Faculty Fellow. In this role, he or she has further opportunity to focus on scholarship while serving as a faculty mentor to his or her colleagues.

Paul N. Markham
Western Kentucky University

The Business of Scholarship

Files and Inventory

Scholars are often too content merely to perform the research, write up the findings, and send the results out into the world. We learned early on that scholarship is a business that demands careful attention to detail in order to make the process both productive and enjoyable.

At the beginning of our career—we've been collaborating for 35 years—we excitedly worked on articles and stories as if each were in a vacuum with a life totally its own. When a piece was finished, we sent it out and began work on the next project. When that one was complete, the process continued. In the early years we kept everything in our heads, knowing that the article on Poe was at *Poe Studies* and the murder mystery was at *Mike Shayne Mystery Magazine.* After a while, however, we had several pieces "out there" and keeping track became more difficult. Our problem really hit home when our chair asked for a report on our scholarly activities, and we couldn't remember where we had sent what, what had been published, what had been accepted, what had been rejected and sent to another potential home. Treasure-hunting for copies of cover letters we may have made was more difficult than Indiana Jones' search for the Ark of the Covenant.

As a result of our near disaster, we decided to be more business-like in our approach. Since then, we have kept a file on each project. To this day we still prefer a hard-copy record of drafts and correspondence even though we store final drafts of articles and stories electronically as well. Each work's file also contains all our research (articles from journals, magazines, and newspapers as well as notes from conversations—complete with dates—along with any other background materials), drafts (always dated to show progress), and correspondences with publications to which the piece has been submitted (also clearly dated). If any question arises concerning the property (e.g., reprint rights), we have a complete record from idea to submission. We even keep our manila files in cabinets marked "In Progress," "Circulating," and "Published" for easy access.

In addition to developing a filing system for our work, we keep an up-to-date inventory of all pieces so at a glance we can tell what's happening to any one piece. We have separate columns for the WORK, WHERE SUBMITTED, WHEN, and DISPOSITION. If an article is rejected, that gets listed; after all, we wouldn't want to send a work back to a rejector by mistake (though we have rewritten submissions in order to comply with our reviewers' suggestions). Since at times we have actually had 30 or 40 pieces circulating at once, such an inventory is invaluable. As we're fond of saying, "Anyone can be the flight controller at the Madison County Airport, but not at O'Hare."

As a side note, we must say with the pride that comes from persistence that just this year we got to move the file for a story that was 20 years old, had been through numerous revisions, and submitted to 14 magazines from "Circulating" to "Published"—all five pounds or so.

Hal Blythe
Charlie Sweet
Eastern Kentucky University

Creating a Survey on Scholarship

Obviously, you have developed your own attitudes about scholarship, but didn't you ever wonder how everybody in your unit (e.g., major, degree program, department, college, university) feels about it? You might be simply curious, you might wish to start a learning community on it, or you might want to determine what, if any, attitudes have to be overcome to increase your unit's scholarship productivity.

One way to find out is to create an online survey through whatever mechanism your institution uses. Don't know much about survey construction? Neither did we when we wanted to find out what our university's attitudes were, so we contacted the Division of Institutional Research and had them walk us through the process. After we made the survey, we sent it out, got an astounding 47% survey response rate, and tallied the responses. Those results helped us figure out what areas we needed to highlight in our faculty development series this year.

One of the biggest obstacles to faculty involvement in the scholarly process we discovered was the differing ways scholarship was supported across campus. For instance, we found that most departments provided some sort of travel funding (usually very meager), but very few offered reassigned time or graduate assistant/clerical staff support to encourage faculty.

Our survey uncovered other major campus obstacles to scholarship. The usual suspects were rounded up—service obligations and lack of blocks of time—but almost everyone admitted to being interested in doing it.

When we looked at those attitudes that promoted scholarship, we found the prime

Shared Tips for the Classroom 51

motivator was self-satisfaction, which confirmed national studies that the strongest cause was internal. Surprisingly, more performed scholarship because they believed it enhanced their teaching than because it was expected. Only a quarter of the faculty thought too much emphasis was put on scholarship.

Armed with the hard data we collected, we now feel more confident in focusing on certain strategies to enhance our campus' faculty development in the area of scholarship. So don't just guess what your colleagues think of scholarship or even rely on anecdotal evidence when you can find out through a survey.

Hal Blythe
Charlie Sweet
Eastern Kentucky University

_____

II. ENHANCING YOUR STUDENTS' SCHOLARSHIP

To continue our metaphor, at the end of the traditional quest, whether it's Beowulf, Arthur, or Indy, the hero passes the knowledge gained through experience to a potential future hero. Likewise, as a scholar, you desire to transmit the breadth and depth of your knowledge to your students.

Sometimes you want to provide your students with a more abstract overview of the scholarly process, and other times you simply wish to offer a necessary skill. Sometimes, as with Odysseus' tutor, Mentor, you become a personal guide to students, either one-on-one or as a group outside of class. Sometimes, you pass on these skills to a classroom of would-be scholars.

This section begins with advice for getting students to start to think like scholars. The next few entries offer help in developing precise skills, such as interviewing and conference presentation. The largest section contains effective classroom methodologies for instilling scholarly skills. The last section concentrates on creating collaborative experiences for students.

So it is that the scholarly quest comes full circle, and we hope that by book's end you will be described as was Chaucer's ultimate scholar, the clerk: "And gladly would he learn and gladly teach."

Promoting Critical Thinking Skills

Thinking Outside the Bag: A Critical Thinking Icebreaker

The first day of class has almost overwhelming challenges: introduce yourself and the class, encourage students to get to know one another through an "icebreaker" type activity, and provide students with some idea about what type of thinking they might actually be doing in class. In response to these challenges, we have created an icebreaker activity that promotes critical thinking and introduces students to the subject matter of the class, as well as each other. In this activity, the professor prepares an assortment of brown paper lunch bag "grab bags," each filled with one small item that somehow relates to the course content. For example, we have used small dollhouse scales, electric candle sized light bulbs, rubber bands, band aids, notes that say "This bag has been left empty on purpose," tiny globes, felt butterflies, a ball of rainbow-colored twine, a mirror, a blank invitation, a toy ladder, a balloon, a kaleidoscope, and a tape measure. In small classes, you will need as many bags as you have students; alternatively, in large classes, students can work together in pairs or triads with one grab bag.

Imagine the students' interest and excitement when they get to come to the front of the room and pick a grab bag for themselves! Immediately, they are returned to their eager 8-year-old selves, shopping for the "best" grab bag at a carnival or dime store, shaking the bag, weighing it with their hand, and curiously guessing what might be inside. After students pick out a grab bag for themselves, they return to their seats and remove the object inside of the bag. They are then given approximately 2-3 minutes to brainstorm by writing to explore the question: *"How could this item be related to the content of the course?"* Students are encouraged to "think out of the box (bag?)" in this activity by using their divergent thinking skills. The answers that students create in response to this question are always richer and more diverse than our initial thoughts of what the item might represent, and have included such things as: systemic, dynamic, culturally diverse, reflective, encouraging listening, balanced, empowering, and risk.

Then students are asked to form groups of four and introduce themselves, the object from their grab bag, and what they think it might represent. Students also brainstorm about the objects in their small groups, thinking of other possible ideas of what the object might represent. Then, they are asked to work collaboratively and use their convergent thinking skills to explore *"How might these four items fit together?"* After this, the students deposit their items on a large table in the front of the room (e.g., the professor's desk). Students are asked to walk by the objects and look at the entire collection. Then the professor asks the small groups to share some of their ideas about how the objects might represent the course content. This component of the activity works best if it is done quickly and with high energy. Because students are thinking creatively and non-linearly, the professor can easily reward and encourage even the shiest student in speaking. Finally, the students return to their groups for a brief discussion and are asked, *"So, what did you learn? What does it matter? How does it affect how you feel about this class?"* Any students who wish to share are asked to do so, but the small groups do not systemically report on their ideas.

We have done this activity with great success in several different psychology courses, including developmental psychology, child psychopathology, and introduction to counseling. Furthermore, the activity lends itself to both graduate and undergraduate courses with equally good results. Adult non-traditional learners have also enjoyed and learned from this activity. Students often report that this activity is one of their favorites of the semester, and that the activity immediately communicated to them that "this class" was going to be something different, fun, and thought provoking.

In regards to Boyer's ideas, the grab bag technique is most closely aligned with the scholarship of discovery and the scholarship of integration. Students are encouraged to discover what the class may be about through brainstorming, seeing familiar items with a fresh set of eyes, and experiencing the joy of creating new ideas. Students also experience the scholarship of integration as they make connections, not only between the objects, but also with how the course might be relevant to their lives, both inside and outside of the classroom. In these micro-experiences of discovery and integration, students are exposed to some of the challenges that await them for the remainder of the semester when they are asked to engage in deeper acts of critical thinking and increasingly sophisticated scholarly work.

DeDe Wohlfarth
Jess Bennett
Laura Gabel
Beth Simon
Dan Sheras
Jody Pimentel
Spalding University

Developing Critical Thinking Skills for Writing

I teach the U.S. History survey. I help students *understand contexts* by examining the many different institutions, beliefs, and life patterns of past human societies and *develop critical thinking* skills so that they are prepared to *reflect and act* as citizens.

My students were assigned to write a paper on Philip Caputo's *A Rumor of War*. Students in my other classes this semester had already submitted reports on another book. The papers indicated that some students were struggling with how to write an essay. The critical thinking skills of many of the students also needed improvement. These earlier papers also indicated that students were not looking at the rubric that I distributed and that some were using Wiki as a source, even though Wiki is often inaccurate.

I designed a different style of instructional guide. I tried to craft something that the students would review. This guide includes graphics as well as instructions on how to incorporate critical thinking into papers. I linked the guide to a rubric. The rubric helped standardize my grading and helped the students improve their writing. Both the writing guide and the rubric will apply to papers that the students write in subsequent courses, so there is portability.

Caryn Neumann
Miami University of Ohio

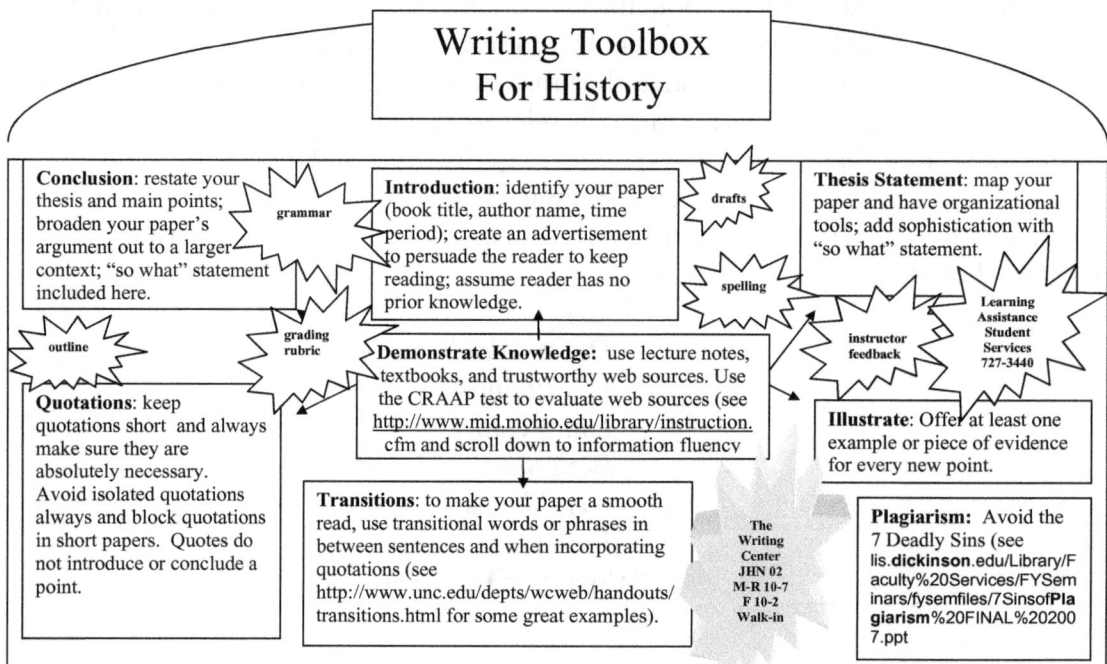

Writing Toolbox For History

Conclusion: restate your thesis and main points; broaden your paper's argument out to a larger context; "so what" statement included here.

grammar

Introduction: identify your paper (book title, author name, time period); create an advertisement to persuade the reader to keep reading; assume reader has no prior knowledge.

drafts

Thesis Statement: map your paper and have organizational tools; add sophistication with "so what" statement.

spelling

outline

grading rubric

Quotations: keep quotations short and always make sure they are absolutely necessary. Avoid isolated quotations always and block quotations in short papers. Quotes do not introduce or conclude a point.

Demonstrate Knowledge: use lecture notes, textbooks, and trustworthy web sources. Use the CRAAP test to evaluate web sources (see http://www.mid.mohio.edu/library/instruction.cfm and scroll down to information fluency

instructor feedback

Learning Assistance Student Services 727-3440

Illustrate: Offer at least one example or piece of evidence for every new point.

Transitions: to make your paper a smooth read, use transitional words or phrases in between sentences and when incorporating quotations (see http://www.unc.edu/depts/wcweb/handouts/transitions.html for some great examples).

The Writing Center JHN 02 M-R 10-7 F 10-2 Walk-in

Plagiarism: Avoid the 7 Deadly Sins (see lis.**dickinson**.edu/Library/Faculty%20Services/FYSeminars/fysemfiles/7SinsofPla**giarism**%20FINAL%202007.ppt

Rubric for Writing Assignments (Keyed to Toolbox)

	Outstanding	Competent	Average	Needs Work	Revision Suggested
Thesis Clarity (20%)	Thesis is clear, argumentative, and acts as an organizing tool for the paper.	The thesis has a clear argument and acts as organizing tool, but could use some rewording for clarity.	Argument is somewhat clear. Thesis could be strengthened by rewording or restructuring. Vague organization for paper is offered.	The thesis attempts an argument, but it is not clear and offers no organization for the paper.	Thesis contains no argument and offers no organization for the paper.
Analysis (40%)	The paper offers a clear and unique analysis that is thoughtfully articulated. Several useful connections are made with course content.	The paper offers a clear analysis of the text that shows comprehension of course content, terms and ideas. Connection made between thesis and course content.	Presents ideas from the course, but some need to be more fully developed. Analysis is attempted and paper attempts to make connections between the thesis and course content.	Presents ideas from course in a basic way. The paper has minimal connection to course content.	Lack of comprehension of course ideas and terms. No connections are made to course content. The paper offers no analysis.
Supporting Evidence (15%)	The paper offers several examples and quotations that support thesis argument. There are no irrelevant quotations and the evidence is balanced. Some outside sources may be present to enhance argument.	The paper offers several examples and various quotations that support and enhance argument outlined in thesis statement.	The paper offers evidence from text, but the evidence is not always clear or relevant and there are claims that may not be adequately supported.	The paper offers minimal evidence, but does support some claims.	The paper has very little evidence. The evidence that is present is confusing and distracts from the argument.
Paper Organization (15%)	The paper is well organized with an informative introduction, good transitions, and a thoughtful conclusion. The paper's organization strengthens the thesis argument.	The paper is pretty well organized. The introduction, transitions, and conclusion clearly connect to the thesis argument.	The paper is somewhat clear and organized, but deviates at times from making connections to the thesis argument.	The paper has clear organizational flaws that distract from the thesis argument.	Has no clear or logical organizational structure.
Grammar and Mechanics (10%)	The sentence structure, grammar, spelling, punctuation, and word choice are intentional and help strengthen the overall paper and argument.	The sentence structure, grammar, spelling, punctuation, and word choice are correct.	An occasional instance of poor sentence structure, grammar, punctuation, and/or word choices and misspellings.	Need to improve the sentence structure, grammar, spelling, punctuation, and/or word choices. There is a pattern of errors in the paper.	Several grammatical and mechanical errors.

Caryn Neumann
Miami University of Ohio

Helping Students Employ the Scholarship of Learning Model

We believe fully in Boyer's four basic areas of scholarship. Above-and-beyond employing those areas in our own teaching, however, is a commitment to assisting students in coming to understand and employ these levels in their own learning. To accomplish this goal, we developed a 4-step model of critical inquiry that, we believe, results in students being able to *integrate* their learning into their lives. The model (see Osborne, Kriese, Tobey and Johnson, under review, for a full description of the model and data on its effectiveness) – which we post in the syllabus and assess in each assignment – includes the following levels:

1.) **Recitation** – state known facts or opinions. A critical component of this step is to acknowledge what aspect(s) of what is being stated is factual and what is based on opinion.

2.) **Exploration** – analyze the roots of those opinions or facts. This step requires digging below the surface of what is believed or known and working to discover the elements that have combined to result in that fact or that opinion.

3.) **Understanding** – involves an awareness of other views and a comprehension of the difference(s) between one's own opinion (and the facts or other opinions upon which that opinion is based) and the opinions of others.

4.) **Appreciation** – means a full awareness of the differences between our views and opinions and those of others. To truly appreciate differences, we must be aware of the nature of those differences. The active dialogue undertaken in the third step (understanding) should lead to an analysis of the opinion as recited by the other. The result should be a complete awareness of the similarities and differences between our own opinions (and the roots of those opinions) and those of the "other."

It is important to acknowledge that "understanding" does not mean to "accept." The goal is not to get everyone to agree; the goal is to get people to truly explore and understand how and why opinions differ. To understand means to realize the circumstances and motivations that lead to differences and to realize that those differences are meaningful. It is our belief that discussing social issues (such as prejudice or racism) without requiring students to explore the roots of their views, to understand the roots of other views, and to appreciate the nature and importance of different views about those issues, perpetuates ignorance. To raise the issue without using the scholarship model may simply reinforce prejudices by giving them voice without question.

We create a scoring rubric and provide these scores to students after each assignment to assess and inform their use of the scholarship of learning. For example, a student post might be assessed for **exploration** using the following scale:

<u>Exploration</u> – analyze the roots of those opinions or facts.
The posts from this student effectively explore roots of opinions or facts

1	2	3	4	5
strongly disagree	somewhat disagree	neither agree	somewhat agree	strongly agree

This rubric provides students with numerical ratings of the degree to which their posted work (this is an online course) demonstrates success on that level of scholarship.

We have gathered data assessing the effectiveness of use of this scholarship model (see Osborne, Kriese, Tobey & Johnson for a full discussion of this work). Raters unaware of student scores on assignments assessed the set of contributions from each student on the four levels of the model. In particular, we were interested in the relationship between student progress on the levels of scholarship and the quality of student interpersonal interactions with other students on the course site (internet course only). We post a 7-level course etiquette description that outlines the kinds of interactions we expect from students in our course. The levels include:

1. respect for others (their viewpoints, their values, their beliefs),
2. the right to disagree but requires sensitivity to the viewpoints of others,
3. taking responsibility for being involved in developing the issues and topics relevant to this course,
4. active participation in all elements of the course,
5. continual feedback to the instructors about the course, course assignments, and individual viewpoints,
6. a commitment to the mutual exchange of ideas. This means we will not isolate definitive "answers" to the issues we raise but we will actively explore and respect the multiple sides to those issues, and
7. a responsibility to "police" ourselves. We are attempting to develop a community and this requires trust. In order to develop trust, we must know that we can share our ideas and not be "attacked." This also requires that we allow other class members the same trust and freedom we expect."

Those students who received the highest scores from the raters on the use of the scholarship levels also received the highest ratings from another set of raters on successful use of course etiquette. In other words, those students who were most likely to progress to the scholarship level of appreciation were also most likely to progress to the level of **responsibility** in their interpersonal interactions with other students in the online classroom.

We use these techniques in an online course on the politics and psychology of hatred. One author uses these same techniques in online courses in Forensic Psychology, History and Theory in Psychology, Social Psychology, and Abnormal Psychology. The other author uses these techniques in a course on political theory and a course on the politics of American ethnic minorities. These courses have been taught face-to-face and online and have had anywhere from 15 to 70 students in each. It seems likely that these same techniques could be employed in courses in any discipline.

Reference

Osborne, R.E., Kriese, P., Tobey, H. & Johnson, E. (under review). Putting it all together: Incorporating "Best Practices" for Teaching Interpersonal and Critical Thinking Skills in an Online Course. *The Journal on Excellence in College Teaching.*

Randall E. Osborne
Texas State University-San Marcos
Paul Kriese
Indiana University East

Using Cognitive Psychology to Teach in Technology

In teaching any subject area, retention is a very important factor. For me as a scholar and technology instructor, retention has an expanded meaning. Not only is retention from the point of view of test performance or measures based on Bloom's Taxonomy important, but the retention of the technical skill after a student leaves campus for gainful employment is also needed. Because so much of the literature in teaching is aimed at testing and achievement, I went outside the realm of education to a similar field, training. The primary difference between education and training comes when the learner needs to apply the knowledge. In training the need is comparatively immediate, whereas in education, the information will be needed at a later time. However, when looking at skill retention for employment, I decided this difference was negligible. It seemed logical that the number of parallels between the fields far outweighed the "time till use" variable.

Plenty of information valuable to technical instruction can be found in training literature. For example, literature from cognitive psychology regarding problem solving and the implications for trainers, entire texts on training transfer with strategies to increase the transfer, and various other tidbits of training literature very closely related to technical instruction abound. Entire journals dedicated to human resource development often have themed issues directly relevant to technical instruction, providing a goldmine of sorts with an almost endless number of veins to investigate.

Because technology topics are often procedural in nature, troubleshooting and problem solving were of particular interest. The review of the literature on these topics provided a wealth of information. Articles regarding troubleshooting techniques, types of troubleshooters, and how to determine each were readily available. However, articles found to be most beneficial referred to literature based in cognitive psychology. This research was particularly linked to areas such as knowledge representation, knowledge acquisition and storage, and problem solving. The literature teemed with information about schema, schemata, mental models, and how the brain retains knowledge. While none of this data was cutting-edge, it was refreshing to look at it through the eyes of a technical educator trying to improve instruction. Immediately the connections between the models of learning and the need to prepare lessons to match these models were apparent. Lessons were rearranged into "chunks," tied to previous knowledge, and other techniques for increasing cognitive learning were applied.

This review of the literature on cognition led to the body of literature on experts and novices. After all, the goal in almost any technical area is to quickly bring a novice to the expert level for maximum performance on the job, post-graduation. After a review of the literature, I conducted a small experiment involving troubleshooting with a failed digital circuit. A novice, an expert, and someone with an intermediate knowledge of digital electronics were invited to troubleshoot the failed circuit. The outcome of the experiment was exactly as found in the literature. The expert was able to solve the problem in the shortest amount of time, but spent the longest time in the diagnosis phase. The novice spent almost no time in diagnosis and immediately began a long testing routine. This experiment was quite refreshing due to the fact that as much time is spent on testing tools and techniques as diagnosis in most discussions of technical troubleshooting.

The review of the literature and the small experiment have reaped far greater rewards than the time required to complete each. Archival materials from the research into this body of knowledge and small experiment have been used over and over in teaching and consulting work. Perhaps most important is the ability to make a case for critical thinking in technical and non-technical settings. Not only does critical thinking follow expert behavior models, but novices frequently lack this skill. In the classroom, characteristics of the expert and novice can be shown to illustrate the importance of modeling the expert. In other classes, a review and discussion of findings from the experiment can be shared. Rather than repeat the experiment, students can be asked to 'imagine' themselves in the experiment and then time can be allocated for a self-reflection of their own methods for troubleshooting. In consulting, technical workers can easily be shown why their time spent on deduction and problem-solving is so critical. This information on expert and novice behaviors has also found its way into service opportunities in offering leadership and supervision training and how it applies in each.

Ray E. Richardson
Eastern Kentucky University

_____

Developing Scholarly Skills

Developing Interviewing Skills

The "real world" needs scholarly thinkers. Complex societal issues, challenging human conditions, and ambiguous ethical situations benefit from bright people thinking deeply about them. But the opposite is also true: academia needs the "real world" to provide us with an opportunity to test our ideas and refine those that have laboratory, but not actual, value. In the process of this applied form of scholarship, a powerful synergy is created, and our students' understanding of problems moves to a deeper level.

The disciplines we teach, clinical psychology and journalism, easily lend themselves to the scholarship of application. Our classrooms are very much like laboratories where students actually practice skills that they will need in the real world. One key skill that cuts across our fields is interviewing. In psychology, clinicians need to develop the skill of quickly connecting with a diverse range of individuals in order to form diagnostic hypotheses and treatment goals. In journalism, writers also need to employ connective communication techniques and active listening skills to decipher information, hearing both what is said and what is not said in order to write perceptive, in-depth articles that accurately convey the reality and context of a story.

To this end, we have begun experimenting with in-class role-play interviewing scenarios that have proven equally successful in undergraduate- and graduate-level classes. In a psychology class (Introduction to Counseling), the professor informs the students that they will be practicing clinical interviewing as a group and they will be interviewing a 16-year-old client with conduct problems in the next five minutes. They are given those minutes to work in small groups and prepare possible interview questions. The professor then leaves the room and, with the aid of a few props, returns as a mohawked, mirror-sunglassed 16-year-old boy wearing an offensive T-shirt. The students' first reaction is to giggle, especially when, for example, they see their middle-aged female professor playing this role. But their giggles soon abate as they realize that the 16-year-old boy is one angry young man with a history of abuse and pain he is willing to share, but only if they, as a class, can build sufficient rapport with him to get him to drop his defiant, profanity-laden persona for a few minutes. The professor stays in character for approximately 20-25 minutes, long enough to force the students to think through various stages of the interview, and they are encouraged to "freeze" the interview and briefly talk openly among themselves as they strategize how to best interview their defiant interviewee. The professor is silent as the students strategize, letting them develop possible solutions to their "problem" client. Students also take notes, as they would during a real clinical interview. Post-interview, the students write up their behavioral observations and interview notes for the clinical interview component of a psychological evaluation, and the result is turned in for an assignment.

In the journalism class (Introductory Magazine Writing), this technique can be used to simulate various in-depth reporting situations. For example, a professor can don a wig, glasses, jewelry, and any other accessories to become the subject of a personality profile. Perhaps the professor is an irate farmer whose generations-old farm is being swallowed by strip-mall development, a grieving parent of a 5-year-old dying of cancer, the owner of the world's largest superhero figurine collection, or the first blind mountaineer to scale Mt. Everest. Again, students are encouraged to talk openly among themselves as they strategize interview questions. The professor-as-interviewee can be alternatively laconic or Robin Williams-esque in his or her pace of speech; the idea, after all, is to teach students to capture the essence of the individual through the compelling questions they ask. As in any interview situation, students are challenged to develop rapport with their interviewee, while also asking thoughtful and sometimes even provoking questions to get the subject to reveal himself or herself. As a follow-up, students use the notes they took during the interview to write short profile articles, and then compare their own attempts to effectively portray their subject with their classmates' efforts.

In both disciplines, the interview follow-up is similar: the professor leaves the room—in essence, breaking character—and returns, somewhat to the students' relief, as him/herself. Then, the professor leads the class in a process-focused group discussion, asking questions such as:

- *What questions worked well? Do you notice any similarities in those types of questions?*
- *What questions did not work well? Do you notice any similarities in those types of questions?*
- *Was the interview what you expected? Why or why not?*
- *What was most challenging for you during the interview? Why?*
- *What was most satisfying during the interview? Why?*
- *Do your notes accurately reflect what was said during the interview? Do they include behavioral observations and physical descriptors?*
- *If you did the interview again, what would you do differently?*

Students have consistently reported that this role-play activity was the most meaningful one of the entire semester, not only because it was memorable, but because it forced them to think critically and quickly, and to think as professionals (psychologists, journalists), and not "just" students. Post-semester, students have approached us and again mentioned how powerful this activity was for their learning, noting the "real world" application of developing interviewing skills for their work in the field.

We believe this technique could be used across a wide range of disciplines, strengthening the connection between intellectual insights and necessary professional skills.

DeDe Wohlfarth
Spalding University
Jenny Wohlfarth
University of Cincinnati

The Interview: A First Foray into Primary Research

In this Internet Age of Student Online Research, students may ignore or fear the process of conducting Primary Research. The ease of e-mail and student enjoyment of its use, however, indicate that the perfect technique for a student's first dabbling in primary research may be in the form of the e-mail interview.

For the past three springs, I have included an interview project in two different courses. Honors 308 – *Women in Music* – is a three credit hour course primarily intended for students in the EKU Honors Program. Music 556 – *Choral Music Literature* – is a three credit hour course for music majors. Both of these courses are small in student enrollment, allowing for a seminar-like atmosphere with extensive student discussion.

The interview project requires each student to conduct an interview via e-mail and report on the answers from the respondent. We examine the information that we receive from the interviews and discuss the responses. The various styles of the respondents are almost as interesting as their actual responses. Some are quite humorous, candid, and extensive. Others are brief and sometimes direct the interviewer to a website. All have given their permission to receive questions prior to the students' receipt of their e-mail addresses.

Steps for the project –
1. Instructor sends e-mail request to possible respondents. After receiving permission for students to contact the respondent, a list of respondents and their e-mail addresses is compiled.

2. As a class, students discuss and describe what they would like to discover from the interviews.
3. Teacher prepares questions that should be included - as guidance for the process.
4. As a group, students devise specific interview questions.
5. Students e-mail interview questions to individual respondents.
6. Students receive answers and assemble results into an oral report.
7. Individual reports are given in class.
8. As a class, the findings are discussed – not as statistical results but empirical research.
9. Results and trends in the responses are noted and compared with secondary research from articles and the class text.
10. Students send thank-you e-mails to respondents.

In three years of my using this assignment in my classrooms, it has proven to be an exciting and fun project. The Women in Music class members interview a professional musician (who happens to be a woman). Professionals from various musical careers are chosen - from composer to conductor to teachers of various ages and levels. The Choral Literature class interviews conductors and composers of choral music. These respondents are chosen to represent various levels and types (academic – children's choirs to college choirs, professional performing organizations, secular, and sacred).

Clearly, the students learn from the responses of the interviews. But perhaps the most important benefits are in the process: the skills in research and critical thinking; responsibility to self, respondent, and class; and question-building, that is, asking in a tactful and concise way what you really want to know. This project can be used in many disciplines and subjects. It may work best in areas that want for immediacy in social, scientific, artistic, or economic thought.

Joyce Hall Wolf
Eastern Kentucky University

Student Scholarship

One of the joys of teaching is trying new activities to provide students with different ways of learning. Often there are unintentional or unexpected outcomes of planned activities that develop, and capitalizing on the unintended is good academic business. In the process of initiating and establishing a partnership with the Library of Congress, American Folklife to join the effort to interview Veterans through the Veterans History Project and involving students in conducting the interviews to meet the Western Kentucky University commitment to increase student engagement, unintentional scholarship also occurred.

The Veterans History Project, enacted by Congress to preserve the history of all veterans involved in war through videotaping to ensure to capture their experiences in their own words unedited for future generations, has met with success and is an ongoing project with partnerships throughout the United States. What began as a specific project that was driven by the sole purpose to interview veterans has been broadened to include scholarship activity through teaching and classroom assignments. Building the videotaping into a class syllabus to encourage students to participate in the Veterans History Project interviewing process was initially difficult as most students did not want to have to go outside the classroom and interview a stranger. Often students declared they never learned how to interview and did not know how to interview.

This tip for scholarship evolved from the Veterans History Project because of the outcomes related to student engagement. To demonstrate that student engagement would increase, a pre vs. post self-administered survey was developed. The results of the survey (ongoing research) demonstrates that there is a statistically significant difference between the self-reported sense of involvement in the interviewing process identified as student engagement among the 56 students who have participated to date in the research. The assessment indicates that the increase had more to do with the videotaping and brief interactive relationship between the student and interviewee than the specific goal for the Veterans History Project. The Veterans History Project was the vehicle for the development of scholarship but not the primary factor.

Scholarship involves the enhanced learning and activities for students, and the call to have students take the risk and learn outside the safe box of academia is encouraged as one means for achieving that enhanced learning. I have found that students value the fact that I actively do interviews and knowing that I am a veteran. I share experiences with the students that include the potential for an interviewee to cry or get upset, and I can with confidence inform students that the interviewees have all volunteered to be interviewed and that I have personally spoken with them prior to the student interview. Students knowing I am not asking them to do something I have not done facilitates their willingness to participate in the videotaping assignment.

Developing an activity or assignment that involves videotaped interviews provides a different dimension for student engagement. I have incorporated interviewing techniques and practice skills related to effective interviewing. The students also receive an Interview Reference sheet that basically gives them questions to ask the interviewee that cover the full spectrum of life. I inform students to conceptualize the full life of the interviewees from where they were born and details of their life prior to entering the military. For the Veterans History Project I tell students to gain as much detail as possible about the military experience, especially war related. The third phase involves life after the military and how it may have changed their life. This format has helped to develop learning beyond just the videotaping that includes the writing of what occurred during the interview in the form of a reflective story with a focus on the before and after feelings experienced by the students. To take this further, providing them with the opportunity to view their own interview in the process of writing their reflective paper allows students to experience learning through the critical assessment of their work.

Students have initially viewed their videotape as a form of self-criticism, and it is essential to set the stage prior to the videotaping and their self-assessment. I challenge students to assess only positive elements of their videotaping and the content of their written reflective paper. I have noted that this is an easy instruction to give but difficult to follow for the majority of students. I provide students with examples of how to focus on the positive aspects. For example, the clarity of the collection of information involves knowing the overall purpose of the interview, knowing how to listen and subtly encouraging the interviewees to open up and share their feelings and thoughts. A number of students require self-practice as they seem so comfortable with assessing what they did wrong or how much better they could have done if they had more practice or another opportunity. I tell students that having the skill to build rapport with the interviewee and to complete the interview demonstrated a high level of skill that is easy to take for granted and that looking closely at all they accomplished is a component of scholarship.

The outcomes for the Veterans History Project have been published in articles such as a front page news story by a journalism student that brought life to her experience and to the interviewee. Regional and national presentations have allowed the sharing of experiences learned and the difference it made to be a part of history, student engagement, and learning from positive assessment. One of the most unique aspects is the desire of students to do another interview or follow-up for more in-depth information that is self-initiated and not linked directly with an academic assignment.

Gary L. Villereal
Western Kentucky University

_____

Decreasing Communication Apprehension by Positive Self Talk: Teaching Students What to Say to Themselves to Reduce Anxiety Before a Presentation

Many students at college suffer from communication apprehension (CA) or the fear of making a presentation/speaking in front of a group (Richmond & McCroskey, 1998). Prior studies on CA interventions have found that several techniques have been helpful in relieving the symptoms of CA (Pribyl, Keaten, & Sakamoto, 2001; Friedrich, Gross, Cunconan, & Lane, 1997). Positive self talk can be very effective in reducing communication apprehension in a short amount of time as it allows the student to think more positively, leading to acting more positively.

Positive self talk or refuting negative thinking is based on Albert Ellis' (1977) premise that individual's make negative statements about themselves. These negative statements or irrational thinking need to be restructured into a more rational or positive thought process for more adaptive thinking. For example, a student who is preparing for a presentation thinks, "If I make a mistake, it will be tragic and I will probably fail the presentation" (negative self talk). The student needs to change these thoughts to a more positive outlook: "When I present and make a mistake, I am going to continue with my presentation as if nothing happened"(positive self talk).

To begin the process of reshaping the student's attitude, the teacher needs to present a brief lecture on irrational and rational thinking, including the following steps:

A. I briefly explain to the students the difference between Negative /Irrational Thoughts and Positive/Rational Thoughts:

Negative/Irrational thoughts are self-defeating thoughts or self-statements relating to an event. For example, a student states, "I **will** look stupid when I talk in front of the class."

Positive/Rational thoughts are thoughts and self-statements that encourage a positive attitude toward an event. For example, a student could change the above negative thought into a more positive thought such as: "Everyone has to present, so I might as well do my best."

B. I also talk briefly about the effects of negative thinking. For example, if a student thinks he or she will look stupid in front of the class, the student may focus thoughts so much on how he or she will look he or she may forget to do part of the assignment.

C. Then I present the worksheet (Appendix A) to the students to complete. This worksheet helps students to think more positively about anxiety-producing events (e.g., making a presentation in front of class).

D. As the students are completing the worksheet, I walk around to make sure all the students understand the assignment. If time permits, getting students in groups to share their responses to the worksheet is advantageous. This group interaction helps start discussions on how positive thinking can impact their schooling/life and how negative thinking can be harmful to their schooling/life.

I was able to use the positive thinking process during a recent undergraduate Abnormal Psychology class. I followed the above steps in talking about positive self-talk and then had the students complete the worksheet (Appendix A). The Abnormal Psychology students were able to identify positive self-statements that led to a reduction in their communication apprehension. I was able to measure their apprehension by giving them a pre-test and a post-test dealing with communication apprehension. The scores from the communication apprehension assessment revealed that as a class their overall communication apprehension decreased. The students verbalized that their thinking was more positive, which led to their being more relaxed and being able to stay focused longer on their communication project.

This attitude-changing process is adaptable to any number of assignments, including those involving research. Helping students develop a more positive attitude toward their abilities can foster confidence to attempt new strategies and delve into more complex subject matter.

References

Ellis, A. (1977). Rational-Emotive Therapy: Research data that supports the clinical and personality hypotheses of RET and other modes of Cognitive-Behavior Therapy. *The Counseling Psychologist, 7,* 2-42.

Friedrich, G., Goss, B., Cunconan, T., & Lane, D. (1997). Systematic desensitization. In J. A. Daly, J. C. McCroskey, J. Ayres, T. Hopf, & D. M. Ayers (Eds.), *Avoiding communication: Shyness, reticence, and communication apprehension* (2nd ed., p. 305-329). Creskill, NJ: Hampton Press.

Richmond, V., & McCroskey, J. (1998). *Communication apprehension, avoidance, and effectiveness.* Scottsdale, AZ: Gorsuch Scarisbrick.

Pribyl, C. B., Keaten, J., & Sakamoto, M. (2001). The effectiveness of a skills-based program in reducing public speaking anxiety. *Japanese Psychological Research, 43,* 148-155.

Jennifer Marshall
University of Cincinnati-Raymond Walters College
Trey Fitch
University of Cincinnati – Clermont College

Appendix A
COGNITIVE INTERVENTION

1. Event that is causing distress:_____
Ex. Presentation in Abnormal Psychology class

2. List the damaging thoughts you might be having in dealing with the upcoming event.
Ex. When I do a presentation, everyone might laugh at me.

a. Negative self-statement dealing with the above event: _____
_____
_____
Ex. I will fail this presentation and forget what I am saying if people laugh at me.

    Is there any support for this thought? _____
    Ex. No support for this thought. No one has laughed at me while I was present-ing.

b. Negative thought #2 dealing with the above event: _____
_____
    Is there any support for this thought? _____

3. List the positive thoughts you might have that refute the above negative thoughts.
Ex. When I present, no one will laugh. I have done presentations before and no one laughed during those presentations.

a. Positive thoughts refuting the above negative thought. _____
_____

    Is there any support for this thought? If so, please list_____
    _____

b. Positive thought #2 refuting the above negative thought. _____
_____

    Is there any support for this thought? If so, please list_____

4. When you are focusing on the positive thoughts before and during the presentation, how will that affect how you act and feel? Be specific.
Ex. I think that if I say to myself everything will be all right and I will make a good grade

---

on this presentation, then that will lead to me being less stressed and more focused.

_____

_____

_____

5. Before your presentation, recite to yourself your answers for 3a and 3b as many times possible.

Ex. When I present, no one will laugh. I have done presentations before, and no one laughed during those presentations.

Class Presentations as a Prelude to Scholarship

What follows is not necessarily a technique introducing scholarship into the class-room, but more a bridge between students seeing themselves as mere students and students seeing themselves as having a stake in the ongoing discussion in a discipline. The objective is to engender the values that lead to genuine scholarship.

I teach philosophy. My principal pedagogical concern is that of establishing a community of inquiry and accountability in the classroom. By this, I mean that students should come to be interested in pursuing discussions regarding class material in a responsible and serious fashion. My means to achieving this goal is by requiring that each student must be the resident representative for at least one view or problem in the classroom. Students are responsible for presenting their assigned view in the best fashion they can. By the end of the semester, every member should have a realm of expertise and have had the opportunity to share it when it bears on an issue at hand.

Students are required to master and present a portion of the course material to the class. For every class meeting, at least one student runs class and presents the issues for a short time. From that time on, that student is our resident expert on that issue. This process creates a sense of ownership of the material. The students feel that some part of the class is theirs, and it is often that I no longer need to correct other students on the issue, as the resident expert is often more than willing to jump in. As such, my classes often reach the point where they are self-regulating. Students keep track as to what's been established, and they become less and less dependent on me to work issues out for them.

Here are some nuts and bolts as to how this process works. First, I have a sheet with dates and issues, and I ask students to sign up for those times for their presentations. As each date draws near, I ask the students presenting to visit my office to discuss the topics. They are required to have done the reading beforehand, and we talk about the material, its implications, and some of the standard worries or objections to the material. Then I ask the student to focus on one issue in the material to present – one argument, one objection, one interesting point. The student is required to write a short (600 word) overview of the issue and read the report for the class at the opening of the next class period. The student is then required to field questions on the issue and run the class for a short (5-10min.) period. I ensure that they will not rely on me or my expertise for that time by asking them to remind me that I am not to contribute while the discussion proceeds.

At first, undergraduates are uneasy with the prospects of presenting material and answering questions from their peers. But slowly, they begin to be comfortable with the idea that they can have well-founded views, too. Often, as class is proceeding, I will ask one of the previous presenters to remind the class about an argument or problem, and soon, they contribute on these points on their own. Classes slowly grow from my univocal presentation of the material to a wide-ranging discussion of the day's reading in light of the issues preceding.

This technique, I have found, has been particularly effective in introduction-level classes in philosophy – the introduction to logic, introduction to ethics, and introduction to philosophy courses. (Vanderbilt's PHIL 100, 105, and 115; WKU's PHIL 100, 320, and 120) Students often come to these courses curious about philosophy, but not sure it is a discipline that can have right or wrong answers. Something they find quickly is that there are most certainly better answers than others, and that they find themselves drawn to represent the better answers as well as they can.

The final stage of this process, however, is where the real payoff is found. The final papers for the course are required to be the students' own work on the arguments, problems, and issues they have presented in class. Many students, because of the regular work they need to do over the semester representing their assigned arguments and problems, have developed sophisticated views on them. As a consequence, the final papers are scholarly, since they reflect a number of months' reflection on the issues. The students tie together the course material to develop comprehensive accounts of how their issue bears in various contexts, fares against standing objections, and is relevant to other concerns in philosophy. Many of the students, by the end of the semester, have impressively worked out final papers. One of the things we discuss in the final class is how scholarship on these issues proceeds and how it grows out of interest in the issues and care for intelligent response to others who care for the issue. The material they worked with to develop their views was assembled for them with my syllabus. The next step is developing the skills and resources to further their research on their own.

Scott F. Aikin
Western Kentucky University

The "I Wonder Why?" Presentation

This tip is being used for several biology classes that I teach, including Anatomy and Physiology, Pharmacology for Dental Hygiene and Pharmacology for Nursing. These are all 200 level courses. For delivery of this activity I use the Discussion Board Forum segment of our course management system (Blackboard). I came upon this idea when students repeatedly asked questions during lecture or class discussions that ultimately I began to group into the "I Wonder Why?" category. As a result of thinking about normal or abnormal physiology, students would naturally think about friends and family with disease processes related to the topic. They posed excellent questions. Initially I would look up the answers if I didn't know them and report back to the students. I quickly realized that the students would benefit from doing this research themselves. As students asked these sorts of questions during the early weeks of the term, I would remind them to write down the questions they asked in class so they could use them for a later assignment. I encouraged the others who did not pose any questions to pay attention to their thought process as they reviewed their material and answered study questions. By the mid-term point I posted the "I Wonder Why?" assignment on the Discussion Board area of Blackboard. I gave clear guidelines for choosing a topic, length and degree of detail expected, and a grading rubric. Students are asked to find 2-3 outside references (credible scientific sources, no Wikipedia or AskJeves). I post an example of quality presentations.

Another part of this exercise is the students' responses to these presentations. Students are expected to respond in a substantive way to 2 different student presentations. The term "substantive" is clearly defined as a response that raises new interesting questions on the topic and seeks to answer one or more of these questions with a summary of their investigation, again using credible scientific sources and summarizing their findings in their own words.

Here is what my general instructions for the IWW presentation look like:

This is a forum designed for your brief presentation on a subject which has caused you, at some point during your study of A & P II, to wonder and to ask questions. Usually such questions which fascinate us are of interest to others as well, and we can all learn much from each others' scientific investigations.

The format I would like you to use in your presentation is as follows:

1. *State the question which you would like to investigate. For example, "Why does hyperglycemia cause vascular damage?" The topic needs to relate to the organ systems we are studying this quarter.*

2. *The format for the presentation is to be a written Word document, one page in length. NO PowerPoint presentations, please. Use scientific references only...no*

Wikipedia, blogs, answers.com or askjeeves type of sources. Please list your sources so that students can do further investigation into your topic.

3. *Be sure to explain the answer to your question in terms of anatomy and physiology; how structure correlates with function. Please be as specific as possible about the actual cellular mechanism of the process you are discussing and relate it to your studies of A & P II.*

4. *Depending on the quality of your paper, you will earn up to 15 points.*

5. *As part of this assignment, whether or not you make a presentation, I expect you to read all the presentations and to make a substantive comment or response to at least 2 presentations. Substantive means that you have questions, comments about the topic or additional information to share or new questions to ask. It means more than "I agree" or "nice job" or "how about those Bengals?" While those comments are welcome, they will not count toward a substantive post. I expect you to pose further questions based on that presentation and to investigate one or more of those questions by doing your own research. I will post examples of quality responses to a presentation.*

6. *When you make your presentation, please start a "new thread" and name it with your last name. When you make a comment about a thread, simply respond to that thread.*

   Please post questions regarding this topic on the same discussion forum. I look forward to reading your questions and your answers. Happy research!

   For proper discussion board etiquette, see this website: http://www.emoderators.com/dltutorial/discussion_board_etiquette.htm

7. *Please look at the examples I have posted which demonstrate a quality IWW presentation and a quality response to a presentation.*

I have discovered that students enjoy exploring their self-generated questions on topics that they care about. They enjoy learning from each other and reading each other's presentations and responses. This exchange generates lively in-class and online discussions based on students' application of foundational knowledge to actual clinical situations. Students can rate each other's posts. Students find this exercise stimulating and enjoyable. They begin to realize that they actually enjoy investigating their own questions using their text and quality scientific sources, training them to become lifelong learners. The anecdotal evidence has been very encouraging. At some point in the future I hope to be able to provide some data to support the effectiveness of this tool.

Ann R. Witham
Raymond Walters College
University of Cincinnati

Employing Effective Methodology

Personal Scholarship as a Model for Taking Class Material Seriously

For students in philosophy classes, there is a lot of writing. One thing that bothered me early in my own undergraduate education was that though the material was still something I was working through, it was not something the teachers themselves were working through at any level. I was writing papers, but they weren't writing much of anything beyond comments on my papers. I found this unnerving – I was being forced to say something about class material, but it looked like the professors themselves had nothing to say. If those teaching the class don't have something to contribute to the discussions between experts, then one of three things is true: this person teaching isn't an expert, there's nothing left to contribute to the discussion, or the discussion is not worth contributing to. For this reason, not only do I actively pursue scholarship in the areas I teach, but I regularly bring it into the classroom. What follows are two relatively simple strategies for integrating your work in the classroom.

The first strategy is to write short popular articles on your area of research. There are not only professional journals for research, but popular magazines, web-zines, newsletters, and so on. I write for a number of these magazines and newsletters. For example, *Scientific American* has a series on Mind and Reasoning, and I regularly submit articles there. Additionally, in philosophy, there is a small number of non-specialist journals designed to bring the esoterica of academic philosophy into common parlance. One in particular is *Think,* and I placed a nice article there on the value of critical thinking. I have my logic students read this essay for the first assignment. I invite my students to try out objections, ask for clarifications, and work out implications with me. It really is great fun – I talk about my research and they get to take pot-shots at me. And in the process, they get to see what a good critical discussion looks like.

The second strategy requires a bit of luck: Be on television or in a documentary as an expert. Granted, these opportunities require that you have the right connections, be at the right place at the right time, and that your area of expertise is something that people would put on television. But when these opportunities do present themselves, jump at them. Not just because it's a little fame coming your way (which is nice), but because it makes for excellent classroom drama. I've been interviewed a few times about the philosophical views at work in the majority's reasoning in *Roe v. Wade*, and in one of the documentaries my interpretation of what the court was up to was presented as definitive both of what the court was up to but also what counts legally. In my ethics course, we read the majority opinion in *Roe* and then we watch selections from the documentary. It is interesting to see student reactions to my presence as an expert – as if to say, "Wow, he really does know what he's talking about!" This places the interpretation and reasoning in the *Roe* case in center stage, and given that the documentary was made with a general audience in mind, all are on-board for the discussion.

There is one drawback to these strategies. Bringing your considered views into the classroom places you squarely on one side of an issue, and risks your being taken to be a partisan both in class discussion and in coursework grading. Students may respond well or poorly to this. On the one hand, having commitments and defending them well is something to be admired and what most students are there to learn. On the other hand, some students may interpret the introduction of your views in the class as extraneous. The teacher should be a neutral guide to the material, and taking a stand on a class issue jeopardizes this. One way I have tried to dispel the impression that these moments of class discussion are overtly partisan is instead of holding the floor when discussing my views, I invite criticism of them. So students who disagree may put me through the wringer instead of feeling as though they've been called out for ostracism. They get to understand positions they reject, they do not feel like they've been indoctrinated, and they have a model for what it is to take the class material seriously.

Scott F. Aikin
Western Kentucky University

Modeling Through Student Writing Communities: A Perfect Scholarly Storm

Several years ago in an attempt to foster a scholarly frame of mind in our upper-division literature students, we began requiring that each student produce a scholarly note (500-1500 words) with an original, researched thesis. To ramp up the importance of the assignment, we required that in addition to handing in the paper for a grade the student had to submit a cover letter for submission of their piece to a specific publication. While we encouraged several students actually to submit their notes and mentored them in revising and submitting during the following semester, we reasoned that the process of research, writing, and planning submission would benefit them all. We taught the process in rather traditional fashion—lecture, discussion, handouts—with, frankly, only modest success. A handful of our students actually saw their notes published, but the overall quality of the papers was a bit disappointing.

Then last year two ideas fortuitously came together in one of those perfect storms for which we all wish. Researching best practices in teaching methodology, we ran across several references to the effectiveness of modeling. Weinstein et al (2002) state, "We can have a tremendous impact helping students develop a useful repertoire of learning strategies. One of the most powerful ways of teaching these strategies is modeling" (277). Further, Weinstein references Pintrich and Green (1994), who claim, "faculty can be models of self-regulated learning.... Therefore, we should strive to model discipline-specific thinking processes and course-specific strategies for learning in our classrooms" (276). And even McKeachie (2002) asserts, "Students are helped by a model of desired performance. This may be provided by the instructor's demonstration of the technique" (255).

Since we were interested in students learning a specific skill—the scholarly frame of mind through production of a publishable note, rather than a pure acquisition of knowledge—we hypothesized that modeling that skill might enhance mastery of it. The problem was how to accomplish this goal. In the past we'd handed out models of our own published notes, but with twenty-plus in our classes we didn't have time to work with each student individually to reveal nuances of technique, etc.

Interestingly, the other "front" in our perfect storm came in the form of a technique we had used successfully in our creative writing courses. Long-time opponents of the workshop approach where the entire class focuses on the work of one student through open discussion, we break our fiction-writing classes into what we call triads. Each triad, or writing community, must meet outside of class to discuss each other's work, and then in a session with us they must present the strengths and weaknesses of the work followed by our comments and an open exchange.

Why not break our lit classes into triads, or scholarly communities, to enhance the writing process! As a trial run, we chose Charlie's American Lit course. Charlie divided his 18 students into six triads. Each triad self-selected around a particular work about which the students wished to write. The students met as a group to discuss the work, parcel out the research, and peer-review each other's drafts. Importantly, each student had to produce a separate note with a distinctively different thesis. We also established a series of progressive due dates so that students had to turn in their basic idea, a summary of a relevant books/articles, another book/article summary, an outline, a first draft, and a final copy in succeeding weeks. This process helped prevent the "write it all the night before" syndrome as did the communal responsibilities.

To model the scholarly process for his students, Charlie asked Hal and a colleague with whom they had co-authored several pieces to join him as a working faculty triad. Charlie, Hal, and Barbara spent the semester modeling—and reporting to the class—

proper procedures as they worked the students through the stages of topic selection, research, drafting/revision, final draft, and submission, always staying a few periods ahead.

Was the experiment a success? Even though all the students haven't heard from their journals at this time, Charlie claims the quality of scholarly notes showed improvement over those of previous semesters. And we might add that our co-authored note on Gilman's "The Yellow Wall-paper" was accepted for publication later this year.

References

McKeachie, Wilbert. "Using Project Methods, Independent Study, and One-on-one Teaching." *McKeachie's Teaching Tips.* Ed. Wilbert McKeachie. 11th ed. Boston: Houghton-Mifflin, 2002. 250-257.

Pintrich, P. R. et al. *Student Motivation, Cognition, and Learning: Essays in Honor of Wilbert McKeachie.* Hillsdale, NJ: Lawrence Erlbaum, 1994.

Weinstein, Clare et al. "Teaching Students How to Learn." *McKeachie's Teaching Tips.* Ed. Wilbert McKeachie. 11th ed. Boston: Houghton Mifflin, 2002: 270-288.

Hal Blythe
Charlie Sweet
Eastern Kentucky University

The Use of Pre and Post Quizzes to Increase Student Engagement in Their Learning

This entry will focus on the scholarship of teaching. As I assume with most educators, I have a constant focus on determining if my students are learning and the quality of their understanding. Specifically, I wanted to increase student retention and understanding by connecting prior learning to current content. Pre-quizzes have emerged as one attempt to answer the above question.

Pre-quizzes developed out of a need to connect once a week classes so that they are much more integrated with each other and not seen as 16 individual units. Pre-quizzes are questions posted on a course management tool or anywhere students have access to them and are designed to keep students engaged in their learning throughout the week and semester. They are called pre-quizzes because they start off each class, and I have used them in all my graduate rehabilitation counseling courses. I create open-ended questions that focus on a review of the last class and questions based on current content. I do not formally grade the quizzes; however, question design and assessment can be tailored to meet the needs of students and instructors. I do collect them a few times during the semester to check student understanding and to monitor if I need to incorporate additional review of the material into the class. I also have students develop and post their own pre-quiz questions. The thought is that the students will ask questions that they are curious about and thus search for their own answers and increase their investment in their learning. Examples of pre-quiz questions are: (1) How is (a course specific concept) related to the philosophy of rehabilitation counseling; (2) Describe something you understand well about the last class; (3) Describe something you are struggling with; (4) What do you see as the benefits of incorporating theory and practice as a future rehabilitation counselor; and (5) What do you see as similarities between Person Centered and Existential counseling? I have also incorporated post-quizzes as a means to summarize current content. Examples of post-quizzes include: (1) Summarize the most important concepts discussed today; (2) What was the most meaningful part of class and why; (3) When you talk to somebody about this class, what will be the first thing you say; and (4) How did today's class meet the objective of this course?

I have not assessed pre-quizzes in a traditional experimental or quasi-experimental fashion; however, I have observed and noted the effectiveness of employing pre-quizzes. First, they have become a method to engage the class in meaningful discussion at the beginning of class. Second, by the student responses I check their level of understanding of content and make on the spot adjustments to class based on their needs. Third, if I believe the students are not preparing for the pre-quiz, I will collect them or have students work in groups to answer the questions—slight changes in the pre-quizzes seem to keep them from becoming busy work. Finally, they act as guiding questions for assigned reading and an anticipatory set for the class. Pre-quizzes have become an integral component to monitoring my teaching and student understanding and engagement in their learning.

The final part of my scholarship is this entry. I am trying to make my efforts public for critique and to build a knowledge base to make teaching more collaborative and less isolated.

Michael Kiener
Maryville University of St. Louis

Micro Embedded Lectures

Aviation evaluation centers around three types of evaluations. They are oral quizzing, the written examination, and the hands-on performance evaluation. This article will concentrate on the evaluation phase involving written examinations. The method I use to develop evaluation instruments is motivated by Boyer's Scholarship of Teaching and

Learning. In the area of aeronautical knowledge and related subject matter testing, aviation educators are taught to use criterion-referenced testing over norm-referenced testing. In the interest of safety, criterion reference testing is preferred because it measures the student's performance against a proficiency standard rather than another student's performance. The written evaluation format includes multiple-choice, true-false, matching, and essay type questions.

Taking into account that time is a limited resource in the teaching process, I aggressively strive to induce learning during all phases of the teaching process, including the evaluation phase. I accomplish this goal by designing test questions that engage students by presenting a last-minute micro lecture embedded in a question when possible. This process results in one last attempt to teach and induce learning even if the student's test preparation was lacking. I have found that this type of question will benefit the student regardless of test preparation by promoting and exposing the student to knowledge. Testing of this nature is a modified building block method that has been used by aviation educators for years. It is predicated on the fact that learning takes place more effectively when going from a given known to an unknown rather than going from an unknown to an unknown. It works well with most testing formats, including oral examinations.

The strategy I employ is simple. I create a narrative in a question which states a fact or facts preceding the question that is directed to the examinee. The question narrative is designed not to give the examinee the answer but rather present a fact related to the required response. In some instances, students have indicated the narrative served as a memory jogger that promoted creative thinking to develop an answer. Even if an incorrect response is recorded, I have found that learning will usually take place. The time required for the extra wording is not an issue. If length is an issue during design of test, I prefer quality over quantity. As an example, I can include an average of 60 teaching points in as little as thirty to fifty questions. This ratio applies to multiple choice, short answer, essay, and even true/false type questions.

The scholarship of teaching involves multiple teaching tasks, all which involve oversight by the teacher. As a teaching tool, I have found that this technique can be a very effective and powerful teaching tool. This technique embraces three phases of the student's learning: pretest preparation, actual test, and participation in a thorough post test review. My goal as an educator is to promote effective learning during each of these teaching phases, including the evaluation phase. I have even used the micro embedded lecture method during oral examinations and practical examinations with positive results.

Based on student feedback and observations during the post-test discussion, the results have been positive. During the post test review, the whole question and not just the intended answer is discussed. Some students have indicated that learning took place even when test preparation on their part was poor. It definitely works for me.

Example Questions and Application

Aviation History

This individual was a brilliant scientist whose work could have changed the entire history of flight-except for one fact. It was 300 years after his death in 1519 before his manuscripts were published and made known to the world. As a result, this knowledge was temporarily lost to mankind and likely delayed the progress of manned flight. Who was this person?

Aviation Technical

This aerodynamic force opposes the downward force of weight on an airplane. It is produced by the dynamic effect of air acting on the airplane wing, and acts perpendicular to the flight path through the wing's center of lift. What is this aerodynamic force called?

Aviation Education

An effective aviation instructor needs a good understanding of the basic characteristics of how people learn so they can be applied in the learning situation. These characteristics are: learning is purposeful, learning is a result of experience, learning is multifaceted, and learning is an active process. Explain the characteristic that states learning is an active process.

Aviation Management Question

The aviation department manager has many administrative, operational, maintenance, and miscellaneous duties to perform. Management skills, especially human resource management skills, are critical to the success of an effective aviation manager. The ability to get things done through people is management whereas being able to influence others is usually considered leadership. Why is effective communication a primary requirement for aviation managers?

Tony Adams
Eastern Kentucky University

_____

Student Developed Test Questions

In a past Principles of Marketing class (undergraduate) I had a number of students who seemed to think that my test questions were unclear and who challenged me several times when I returned the first test. I decided to allow the students to write the next test. This is what I did.

1. Each student in the class had to develop five multiple choice questions out of an assigned chapter. (I had planned to cover 5 chapters, so I divided the class into fifths and assigned the same number of students to each chapter.)

2. I took up the questions and selected an appropriate number for the test and eliminated duplicates.
3. When the test was copied, the name of the student who had written the selected question appeared next to question.
4. When I graded and returned the test, if someone challenged a question, the student who wrote it had to defend his or her question.

This strategy turned out to be a very positive thing — not because of the confrontations that took place (and some certainly did!) but because the students had to really THINK about not only how to write the question but also the background knowledge and scholarship necessary to defend it and why each of the incorrect answers was incorrect. It also had the added benefit of allowing the students to take pride in their own writing skills — and it showed them that a great deal of thought and art goes into designing tests.

S.J. Garner
Eastern Kentucky University

Measuring Student Self-Confidence

Our feelings are our most genuine paths to knowledge
—Audre Lorde

Teachers can sometimes overlook the validity and usefulness of measuring student attitudes. Measuring student perception will not sufficiently determine if student X can name part Y, but courses often have other, more lofty goals, such as "this course will prepare the student for the workplace" or "students in this course will become self-directed learners." Measuring student confidence about various situations can yield fascinating—and very useful—data. For example, one of the goals for our institution's upper-level capstone course in software engineering is that students would, by the end of the class, have the skills needed to be successful in the workforce. Pre- and post-tests were used to analyze how certain course activities influenced students' confidence about situations they are likely to face in the "real world." The tests asked questions such as:

- I feel comfortable working and participating in small groups.
- I feel comfortable in asking probing questions that clarify facts, concepts, or relationships.
- I am flexible and creative in seeking potential solutions to problems.

- I am primarily responsible for my own learning.
- I am willing to persevere and persist at finding solutions to problems.
- I am most concerned with finding the right answer to an issue or problem.
- I am curious about how and why things work.
- I value different points of view.
- I am confident in my ability to identify and search for information needed to solve a problem.
- I like working with problems that have many solutions.

   Measuring the mean differences between pre- and post-tests on these questions has shown that certain classroom exercises (experiential learning activities) change student attitudes toward situations and activities they will find in the workplace.

Carol Lushbough
Asai Asaithambi
Bruce Kelley
The University of South Dakota

End-of-Course Review Paper Utilizing a Novel

   There are many kinds of writing assignments. John C. Dean in *Engaging Ideas* has catalogued more than three dozen personal and professional writing activities that faculty can assign to students. One formal writing assignment that has worked well for me many times is an end-of-course paper over a provocative novel that requires students to integrate lecture and other course material. The assignment also serves as a comprehensive review for the Final Exam and a means of assessing student comprehension of course content.

   While I have used this general assignment in other courses with different novels (for example, Margaret Atwood's *The Handmaid's Tale* in a course involving civil rights and civil liberties), here I focus on my upper-level undergraduate political interest groups course enrolled primarily by political science majors who on the basis of previous coursework have a solid grounding in the discipline. Specifically, I utilize a writing assignment over a satirical novel, *Thank You for Smoking* by Christopher Buckley, as an analytical exercise to improve and evaluate student comprehension and as a way to make a political interest groups course more enjoyable for students.

   When employing a novel as the basis for a comprehensive review writing assignment, one must realize that the book chosen is critical to the exercise. To the maximum degree possible it should "fit" course content, be "rich" in detail, and be interesting to students. The key is to give students a novel that they can compare and contrast productively with other material in the course. *Thank You for Smoking* (*TYFS*) is well-written, very funny, and full of references to contemporary American politics. The story centers on Nick Naylor, the chief spokesperson for the Academy of Tobacco Studies (ATS), the tobacco lobby. A partial list of Naylor's activities includes: multiple appearances on TV talk shows, interacting with print journalists, testifying before Congress, social lobbying, announcing goodwill public relations campaigns, attacking political opponents, delivering hush money, discussing campaign contributions, influencing the content of public service advertising, arranging product placement in a Hollywood movie, ghost writing op-ed pieces and congressional testimony, commiserating with other lobbyists, cultivating contacts with legislators, presenting research and technical information, meeting with front groups, and using reverse psychology on a foreign leader. Along the way, Buckley provides a mostly accurate, thought-provoking picture of lobbyists, political interest group strategies and tactics, media campaigns, Congress, and policymaking.

Over the course of a semester in lectures and assigned readings I convey to students that there are many different kinds of political interest groups at the local and national levels (corporations, peak business associations, trade associations, professional associations, unions, nonprofits, cause groups, public interest groups, institutions, governments, etc.); that such organizations fulfill several important functions in the political system (representation, education, participation, etc.); that different categories of lobbyists (ex-Congresspersons and other former government officials, lawyer-lobbyists, public relations lobbyists, associational lobbyists, etc.) are involved; that many different roles are performed by these actors (contact person, political strategist, liaison lobbyist, advocate, public spokesperson, etc.); and that many different kinds of political behaviors are used by political interest groups (contacting government officials, testifying before Congress, organizing grass roots lobbying campaigns, interacting with the media, contributing money to candidates, protesting, litigating, etc.). I also cover topics related to the career paths of lobbyists, the motivations of private sector lobbyists versus public interest lobbyists, the characteristics of good lobbyists (knowledgeable, high ethical standards, adaptable, etc.), rules for effective lobbying (credibility, compromise, don't burn bridges, etc.), and the strategies and tactics, including media campaigns, used by political interest groups in interacting with political institutions, such as Congress and the public. I explain that all this material, plus the novel, is the raw material from which they have to craft their paper.

I ask students to consider the following question as the basis for a medium-sized paper (roughly ten pages double-spaced) at the end of an academic term:

> To what degree does Christopher Buckley's fictional slice-of-life account of Academy of Tobacco Studies' lobbyist Nick Naylor provide an accurate portrayal of the job of a lobbyist and the politics of lobbying in America?

The assignment requires students to evaluate comprehensively the specifics of the Nick Naylor saga in terms of where it conforms to and where it deviates from what they have learned about political interest groups over a semester. Hundreds of papers and many class discussions have demonstrated that students are able to separate fiction from fact.

The assignment works well because the details contained in the novel match-up well with the canon of knowledge political scientists have about lobbying and lobbyists. By examining the characters, especially Nick, and the actions portrayed in the novel, students can make many connections to the material in a political interest groups course. Thoughtful undergraduate students have proved capable of reaching conclusions and providing supporting evidence regarding (a) the unique nature of tobacco as an interest and the ATS as an organization; (b) the career path of Nick compared to real lobbyists; (c) system functions, positive and negative, that ATS performed; (d) Nick's motivations and personal dilemmas as a lobbyist; (e) the degree to which Nick possesses the "good" characteristics of lobbyists; (f) identification of Nick as a lobbyist-type; (g) categorization of specific political behaviors, strategies, and tactics used by political interest groups; (h) the relative emphasis on direct versus indirect lobbying; (i) the types of media campaigns Nick orchestrates; (j) degree of conformity to various "rules" for effective lobbying; and (k) an overall judgment regarding the pedagogical value of the novel. An abundance of material exists with which students can work in writing their individual response to the assignment.

Students are more likely to learn concepts when they find course materials interesting and assignments challenging. An end-of-course review paper incorporating a good, enjoyable novel is one way to accomplish this purpose while also preparing students for the Final Exam and providing the instructor with another measure of what students learned during the course.

Clyde Brown
Miami University

———————————

Meditation: A Technique for Enhancing Scholarship

The amount of information on the subject of meditation and classroom performance has been increasing. A number of articles report that there appears to be a connection between meditation and increased concentration among students. Discussions about how meditation encourages a sense of discovery and inquiry of knowledge have also appeared. An article entitled "Transcendental Meditation Helps Students," published in the *International Herald Tribune*, reported that Research on Transcendental Meditation practices in U.S. schools shows improvement in the concentration of students (Micucci, 2005). Gary Kaplan, a neurologist and clinical associate professor of neurology at New York University School of Medicine, in the same article, reported that "Transcendental Meditation . . . produces a state of restful alertness that provides the body with deep, rejuvenating rest and allows the mind to reach higher levels of creativity, clarity, and intelligence" (2005, p. 1).

As a college faculty member, I have discovered over the last two decades that meditation enhances scholarship by encouraging concentration, inquiry, discovery, and a deeper examination of knowledge. I employ meditation at the beginning of my undergraduate classes in order to engage each student in the benefits of learning how one can train the mind to obey mental commands that shape and control a person's thoughts. I introduce students to techniques that enable them to expand their consciousness and create a sense of concentration—a much needed ingredient in the learning process. Hence, I have discovered that mediation is a tool that professors can use to prepare students, engaging them in deeper learning by allowing meditation to set the stage for alertness and receptivity. I have found that meditation benefits students with improved mental performance, improved creativity, improved problem solving, and improved memory by seeking deeper meaning of knowledge and clearer thinking. Additionally, I have observed some students in my classes demonstrating what I believe to be improved concentration after performing meditation. If nothing else, the act of meditating at the beginning of class has a certain mystique that causes some students to model a more serious attitude about the content.

The process that I use is quite simple. I do not employ any scientific systems or formal methods of meditation. For instance, I do not require students to learn the methods of Transcendental Meditation, nor do I insist that my students study the lessons of Raja Yoga; however, I suggest to them that these formal methods may serve a valuable purpose to individuals who are seeking an in-depth knowledge of the classic meditation practices. For the purpose of my class, I try to get students ready for the session's activities by providing them with a comfortable way to relax and prepare their minds for class discussions. I do that by asking them to take a few minutes to engage in a short, five-minute meditation exercise.

I conduct the exercise in a very simple format. After the students are seated and the attendance has been taken, I instruct the students who can to sit quietly in a comfortable position with their backs straight, their heads extended straight, their shoulders relaxed, and their eyes closed. I then instruct the students to breathe comfortably through their nose, inhaling to the rhythm of their heartbeat, and to exhale in the same fashion. While they are engaging in this process, I give them some mental affirmations to silently repeat. These affirmations are mental suggestions, positive words to repeat that I interject during their meditation practices in order to guide their thoughts and to assist them in reaching what I call the "readiness stage of learning." Repeating these sayings silently while breathing has a tendency to help stop the mind from wandering. I remind the students to relax and try to discharge all of the chatter in their minds. The key to this exercise is to encourage the students to relax and focus on the joy of learning and not become anxious, fearful, or uncomfortable.

Breathing and concentration are two important aspects of this exercise that I encourage students to master. Meditation requires proper breathing in order for the body and mind to be in harmony—relaxed and comfortable. And, the mind should be trained to concentrate on one thought at a time. I remember when I first started using meditation as a tool in the classroom: I told the students that I read that an untrained mind is like a dog that has been restricted to a cage over a long period of time. When the cage door opens, the dog runs wild and uncontrollably. I told the students that, to a large extent, the untrained human mind is also like a caged dog. With worry, fear, anxiety, and stress, the mind is caged up. When freed, the mind will wander uncontrollably from thought-to-thought and chatter-to-chatter if it is not trained. Meditation is one tool that can be employed in order to discipline and train the mind to conform to a state of ease and relaxation.

In summation, I have experienced that meditation is beneficial—to the professor and to the students. Practicing meditation as a tool for enhancing knowledge and developing successful intelligence is worthwhile. Meditating before conducting class activities has positive effects. Central to meditating at the beginning of class is the process of relaxing one's mind and preparing for the activities, discussions, and exercises that will be presented in the class. Attaining a sense of relaxation in class has proven results; among them are the will to focus and concentrate on classroom materials and the readiness to acquire new knowledge in a broader sense of investigation. Meditation is a simple and straightforward way to get the most out of every student in every class setting—and, it works for me.

Reference

Micucci, D. (2005, February 15). Transcendental Meditation helps students. Herald International Tribune, p. 1.

Sherwood Thompson
Eastern Kentucky University

_____

Creativity & Inspiration: An Interdisciplinary Approach to Engaging Pre Service Teachers

The instructor's focus in the class, Social and Emotional Development in Middle Level Curriculum, was to provide the instructional foundation and foster planning for social, emotional, intellectual, and physical growth in middle level adolescents, providing classroom management strategies appropriate for this age-group. Practicum block experience was taken along with this class. This course was designed to provide a psychological basis for working with middle level students.

The desired outcomes of the class were to:
* Develop lifelong learning practices in students, including self-evaluation skills.
* Demonstrate/exhibit compassion and sensitivity to students of all cultures.
* Demonstrate knowledge of facts and an understanding of fundamental principles, ideas and relationship among various knowledge domains.
* Demonstrate knowledge of past and present developments, issues, research, and social influences in the field of education.

Theoretical Framework for Using Technology

In expanding our concept of scholarship, Boyer's seminal *Scholarship Reconsidered: Priorities of the Professoriate* (1990) illustrates a model for scholarship encompassing four basic areas: discovery, integration, application and teaching. Pat Hutchings and Lee Shulman (1999) argue that not only does scholarship dictate an attitude of inquiry, but that it requires making one's research public so that colleagues can review it according to accepted standards for critique and for building upon. In this sense, scholarship, for both the instructor and the student, is a process of active discovery where teaching is a vehicle of instruction.

At the same time, Laura Richlin (2006) states that "Scholarly teaching and the Scholarship of Teaching and Learning (SoTL) are closely interrelated, but they differ in both their intent and product. Because both are vital to the life of the academy, it is necessary to clarify and operationalize each of them."

In the class, active learning became an integral part of the learning environment due to the variety of majors. In addition, because of this diversity, students engaged in collaborative learning. The use of emerging technologies allowed hands-on training and skills transfer, while providing an interactive forum for discussion about problems adolescents face in middle schools. The procedures outlined below will enable students to view issues and problems through other students' lenses, a blurring of disciplinary lines.

Believing that each student is a clean slate, rather than assuming that they have the same body of knowledge, the instructor incorporated different learning styles and varied modalities.

Outline of Activity

The use of emerging technologies in conjunction with the class syllabus and rubrics is outlined below:

1. **Article Reviews:** Students are to read two articles on problems adolescents face, and write a review of each article and submit written reviews to the online article File Star database. Each review consists of (1) article summary, (2) prior knowledge of issue, (3) connections to classroom discussion, and (4) general overall critique/reflection of the article.

2. **Problem Paper:** Students are required to research a problem adolescents face, with prior approval from the instructor. The students then develop a problem paper and 10-15 minute PowerPoint presentation. The presentations will be video-recorded, compiled onto a DVD and distributed to all students.

3. **Partner Advisory Unit:** Students are partnered and required to develop a plan for ten lessons in a two week unit. The Partner Advisory Unit is also video-recorded. After an introductory training session on iMovie, the students edit their videos and compile their presentations onto a DVD which is distributed to the class.

Effectiveness of using Technology in this context

1. Article Reviews

The students' prior knowledge enabled them to make connections throughout their literature reviews. The online database of article reviews requires special programming language (code for italicize, bold and underline), indirectly teaching students how to format papers according to APA 5th Edition style.

Along with this class, students are required to undergo practicum experience, going into local schools for four weeks to observe middle-school students. While they were researching problems adolescents face, and discussing their peers' presentations, the students were able to make connections, alluding to Boyer's first basic area, that of discovery.

The students began to sound like graduate students, using research terminology and even in some cases, correctly identifying disorders, and problems with their own students, making connections through research, practical application and discovery.

2. iMovie for Student Presentations and Partner Advisory Unit

First, it was necessary to teach the students the software program (iMovie). Providing them with this foundation allowed the students to progress creatively and to think critically.

The DVDs provided documentation of their research, a validation of their work. First, these presentations allowed students to judge themselves objectively and note their presentation weaknesses. These activities additionally enabled pre-service teachers to start expanding their own knowledge base by providing research and resources that they can use in their own classrooms. Here, learning beyond the textbook became evident. Recorded student presentations both verified and validated rubric scores, allowing students to evaluate and compare presentations. Finally, having the ability to record a presentation allowed the instructor and students alike to concentrate on the presented material, instead of taking notes.

The iMovie hands-on training allowed the students to move enthusiastically beyond the textbook, whereas the traditional textbook and lecture process limits creativity and curiosity. The students created video clips as teaching instruments for the classroom, which integrated well with their presentations. These students had a passion for their topics, discovered a purpose, and developed a plan, positioning themselves for success.

Tips for Each Activity

Literature Reviews

1. Have an online database for article reviews.
2. Provide an example of a good article review.
3. Be clear in directions for online data basing.
4. Provide students with language (coding).

Recording Presentations: Problem Paper and Partner Advisory Unit

1. Provide a rubric and necessary examples.
2. Ensure a power supply for recording presentations.
3. Have a tripod for stability and quality.
4. Be familiar with media and equipment.
5. Reinforce presentation time limit.
6. Ask for a volunteer to record presentations.
7. Make sure that the room is conducive to recording.
8. Record one student presentation per disc/ tape.

Making an iMovie and Preparing DVDs

1. Determine where and when students can train.
2. Make sure computers have adequate memory as well as DVD burning ability.

3. Introduce software to students with a simple project initially.
4. Download the video clips to computer hard-drive.
5. Once students have downloaded the files, they must edit the video.
6. Any text or background music needs to be collected, ideally ahead of time.
7. Burning DVDs takes time. From creating an iMovie to iDVD, the whole procedure (PROCESS = RENDER = BURN) is time-consuming!
8. Have students prepare the presentation as an iMovie themselves.
9. Try to get server space where they work on their own student presentation.

References

Boyer, E. L. (1990) *Scholarship Reconsidered: Priorities of the Professiorate* Princeton, New Jersey: Princeton University Press, The Carnegie Foundation for the Advancement of Teaching.

Hutchings, P. & L. Shulman. (1999) The Scholarship of Teaching: New Elaborations, New Developments. *Change, 31* (5), 10-15.

Richlin, L. (2006) *Blueprint for Learning: Constructing College Courses to Facilitate, Assess and Document Learning.* Sterling, VA: Stylus Publishing, LLC.

Mildred M. Pearson
Krishna Thomas
Bev Cruse
Eastern Illinois University

Scholarship and Caring in Advanced Pediatric Assessment

Mastering the art of advanced pediatric physical assessment is challenging for even the most experienced Registered Nurse (RN). Achieving an acceptable comfort and competence level as a beginning nurse practitioner and primary care provider is particularly daunting, especially for those nurses who are not comfortable caring for children. Recently I discovered a process that allowed me not only to incorporate the concepts of scholarship and evidence based practice into an intensive 3 day on campus experience but also to increase comfort with pediatric advanced assessment skills and techniques while adding to the joy and pleasure of caring for children and their families as they started their process of becoming advanced practice nurses (APNs).

My discovery process started when I was assigned the task of providing the students with essential pediatric assessment information and essential concepts needed as they begin clinical experiences with community-based preceptors. Recognizing that I would be unable to go into a comprehensive presentation in the allotted 2 hours, I first pulled together my "Essentials List" of "need to know" information and resources. My e-list consisted of broad topic headings including the major developmental milestones, body system and assessment techniques consistent with typical challenges children present with in primary care health care settings. Additionally, I located and added easily accessible online and hard copy evidence-based resources coinciding with each major topic and concept to my presentation the students' future reference.

On the day of the presentation, I introduced myself and outlined what we would discuss during our time together. The first topic we covered was the concept of being a Nurse Detective and hunting down the information they needed to take care of kids. I also asked a series of questions to break the palpable tension in the room. The questions were, "Are you sure you are in the right place? How many of you take care of sick and injured children on a daily basis? Regularly? Occasionally? How many of you have children? ....and finally, How many of you were children?" After breaking the tension with a laugh and recognizing that a handful of positive responses were garnered with each preceding question (until the last one), I outlined the concept of the tools they possessed to help them take care of their younger patients. During the first 5 minutes of our time together, I asked them to shout out what, if anything, they felt unsure about when assessing children and adolescents. The topics were broad and varied from health promotion concerns to specific disease management processes. I thanked them as I wrote them all down and told them that during our allotted time we would discuss where in the literature they could find resources for any answers to any questions that would not be addressed during our time together.

As we discussed the importance of knowing the "rules of the road regarding pediatric health assessment" and general guidelines for the concepts of growth and development, I handed each one a document with a series of trigger phrases and urls correlating to each body system and pediatric assessment knowledge point. As we progressed through the body systems, developmental findings for the different ages and stages and body system differences from adults, I stressed the importance of finding the most current research, peer-reviewed source and gold standard guidelines to guide their critical thinking. We had discussions on typical assessment findings, and I briefly highlighted each body system and the corresponding online and hard copy resources listed on their handout that could help guide their treatment and plan of care, including interventions, medications, laboratory and x-ray studies, along with invasive and noninvasive procedures and treatment options.

During the last 45 minutes of our time together one of the students was gracious enough to offer his own children (his family having come with him for the 3-day on-campus experience) as "models." I was able to demonstrate brief physical assessments on his 2-month-old son and 18-month-old daughter along with a brief Denver Developmental standardized test. The students were also fortunate to have the opportunity to interact and observe "stranger anxiety" (a normal developmental finding) in the 18-month-old daughter. Serendipitously, several of the students established rapport with the older little girl and played "catch" with her along with performing a brief physical assessment as well. While the students were playing and examining her, the entire group was lucky enough to observe this student-child interaction and how the students (who had worked in pediatric care settings and had several children of their own) had a comfort level in caring for children and what a difference this made in creating a pleasant environment and examination experience for everyone involved. In future intensive presentations I will include additional "live model" activities to reinforce, demonstrate and give students the opportunity for brief "hands-on" interaction with children and their respective families.

The written pediatric assessment student evaluations were positive, and individual verbal comments from students ranged from: "...I thought I didn't like kids, but maybe they're not so bad...,"and "I really never cared for children but being able to know where to find "kid" information helps...," to "...never really thought about being a "detective" but it makes sense... finding current research to support what I'm thinking...makes me feel better..." Based on my positive experience with this intensive "boot camp" type experience and favorable student evaluations, I will definitely continue to find ways to include more emphasis on weaving scholarship (using current research) into all of my future advanced practice pediatric assessment didactic and clinical presentations.

Wrennah L. Gabbert
Texas Tech University

_____

Using the Scholarship of Discovery to Enhance Classroom Teaching and Student Learning

The scientific method is the foundation for the scholarship of discovery in the physical, life, and social sciences. The efficacy of this ubiquitous model rests on the balance it strikes between two different cognitive processes: deduction and induction. Scientists use deduction to design experiments and plan their observations of the natural world. Theories are the conceptual frameworks scientists use as guides to simplifying the world's bewildering complexity so that the relationships between important variables become more salient. The goal of deduction is simplification and control. In contrast, induction involves analyzing evidence from observation and synthesizing it with broad general theories. Induction is largely an integrative process; particulars of individual experience and observation are combined to develop and refine broader explanatory structures.

While the model of the scientific method is used throughout the sciences, its application to the scholarship of teaching and learning has been limited. Often the process of learning is conceptualized as the simple transfer of information from the teacher and text to the mind of the student. All too often, the effectiveness of this process is measured solely by students' ability to reproduce accurately knowledge previously received. However, if one understands that learning is a dynamic process as well as the passive reception and storage of knowledge, the value of applying the scientific method to the design of courses becomes more apparent. In particular we suggest faculty design classroom experiences that require students to actively experience, observe, record, reflect and synthesize material related to the course of study.

An Introduction to the Behavioral Sciences is a sophomore-level course which introduces students at Berea College to three behavioral sciences: anthropology, sociology, and psychology. The teacher and teaching assistants have worked together over the last year to enrich the course by designing multiple direct learning experiences for students in the course through the use of deduction. Through a variety of individual and group assignments and activities, students learn through primarily inductive processes to create meaningful knowledge structures.

Like some other classes, this course used daily quizzes to reward students for reading the assigned material regularly. Unlike most classes, however, the quizzes also allowed students to expand their understanding of the material and develop important scientific skills. After all students completed the quiz, their individual answers were collected, students were randomly assigned to groups of 3 or 4 and asked to re-accomplish the quiz they had just completed. Students' grades were the average of their score on the individual and group quizzes; all students in each group were allowed only a single answer to each question. In the small group, students relied on what they remembered from the reading but they also needed to learn when to argue for their answers and when to defer if a classmate presented a more persuasive argument or better evidence for an alternative answer. This experience helped students understand the importance of using evidence and reasoning logically to reach consensus.

Students were also given two group assignments during the semester. On both occasions students were introduced to a theory then viewed a popular film using the frame provided by the theory to identify instances relevant to theoretical components. For sociology, students viewed *Crash* and applied aspects of Merton's sociological theory of anomie. For psychology, they viewed *One Flew Over the Cuckoo's Nest* and identified examples of the five perspectives of psychology used in an introductory psychology text. On both occasions students and their group members gave a presentation to the class on the evidence found in the movie pertaining to their assigned aspect of the theory.

To help students experience what they were learning, we also used several "games." Two of these were *Sociopoly* and *Colourblind*. *Sociopoly* is played on a regular monopoly board but initial assets are distributed in a way similar to the actual distribution of wealth in America. The Banker, representing the top quintile, not only gets well over half of the total wealth distributed but is encouraged by the private instructions to make up and enforce whatever rules s/he feels are necessary and appropriate. *Colourblind* requires students to work together to identify the pieces missing from a 30-piece conceptual matrix. These games, as well as other classroom demonstrations and activities repeatedly challenged students to use what they had learned about the scientific method to understand and learn from their actual experiences.

The course was culminated with a student learning portfolio, which included evidence of all the students' activities during the course. The portfolio included essays by the students describing what they did and what they had learned from the quizzes, activities, discussions, group projects and the experience of the course as a whole. Students were asked to assess and analyze their own understanding of the scientific method and its centrality to the behavioral sciences.

Of the 68 students who enrolled in one of the first three sections of the course, four withdrew but the other 64 all earned grades of C or better. All items were rated at or above the campus averages on the institution-wide end-of-course critique. In particular, students' ratings of the time they spent studying, the extent to which the course helped them think more critically, provided clear objectives and fair grading, and effectively enhanced their learning were more than .5 standard deviations above the campus mean. Several excerpts from student reflections help illustrate students' positive response to the course:

- ...because we had quizzes almost every day of class, I knew I had to do the reading. There was no bull-crapping the quizzes either. This isn't stuff you can just make up.
- This class is probably the most interesting class I have ever taken... great readings, movies, and class activities.
- This course has taught me not just about behavioral sciences but about myself as well.
- This course was probably the single most important class I have taken in my entire life. It completely shook up my beliefs and what I thought to be true and forced me to examine everything under a new light. I had to prepare every day and take an active part in class.

Dave Porter
Megan Rodgers
Kaleigh McCoy
Berea College

_____

Exploring Cultural Diversity with Pre-service Secondary Teachers Using "My Life in a Bag"

As teacher educators we have the responsibility to prepare teachers to become culturally responsive educators who are able to "demonstrate the content, pedagogical and professional knowledge, skills, and dispositions necessary to help all students learn" (NCATE, 2008). I teach *Adolescent Growth and Development,* a required course designed to assist undergraduate students to understand the physical, social, and cognitive development of adolescents. I have infused the course with various activities designed to help these pre-service secondary teachers think about their future students as cultural resources, providing them with rich information to design developmentally and culturally relevant instruction that is motivating and engaging to their future adolescent students. One activity that facilitates an increased awareness of cultural diversity and one that the pre-service teachers may actually use in their future classrooms to learn about their own students is "My Life in a Bag," an activity originally created by Dr. John Caruso at Western Connecticut State University.

In preparation for this activity, I ask the students to think about the term "culture" and brainstorm what culture means to them. After recording and discussing their responses, I then share the following definition:

> Culture is a system of norms, standards, and control mechanisms with which members of society assign meanings, values, and significance of things, events, and behaviors; culture includes patterns of knowledge, skills, behaviors, attitudes, and beliefs, as well as material artifacts produced by human society and transmitted from one generation to another (Pai, Adler, & Shadiow, 2006, p. 239).

For homework students are instructed to locate and place 5 items in a small bag that reflect their cultural identity. If an item is too large to place in their bag, they may bring a photo or description of it on an index card and place it in the bag. They are to bring the bag and a blank sheet of paper with their name written on it to the next class. On the day of the activity, students form small groups of 4-6 students and identify a partner in their group about whom they know the least. They switch bags and the paper with their name on it with their partner and without discussing the items, review the artifacts in their partner's bag and write down how they think each item represents their partner and his/her culture.

After students have written their perceptions of their partners' artifacts, they then switch the bags and papers and read what their partner wrote. Then, still within their small cooperative learning group, each individual then shares his/her own artifacts with the group and describes how each item represents his/her cultural identity. After allowing time for the group members to share their cultural artifacts, I then facilitate a large group discussion asking students to share comments about the activity, including any misconceptions about their partners' artifacts and how initial impressions could lead to stereotyping and misunderstanding. We also discuss how they may use this activity to learn about their own students so that they are able to incorporate aspects of their future students' cultures into the design of their instruction to make learning meaningful and engaging for all of their students within their content area.

For homework and as a test grade, the students are to write a seven-paragraph essay (including an introduction and conclusion) describing their own five items and how each represents their culture. I grade the written essays using a scoring rubric assessing content, organization, style/tone/language, and grammar/punctuation/mechanics. The reflective essays are rich with valuable information about the students as individuals, their writing ability, as well as their disposition for teaching.

Frequently included items in the cultural bags are photos of family, pets, and friends. Other popular items are regional religious artifacts, such as crosses and rosaries. Representations of music are often included, such as music CD's as well as other popular technologies such as iPods, cell phones, computers, and games. Students often place items representative of their passions, such as sports memorabilia, hobbies, etc. Most students include some reference to their ethnic heritage. For example, one student included a flag of Lebanon "to represent my Lebanese heritage" and the flag of Ireland "to represent my Irish heritage." Cultural references to food are often included:

> My grandparents on both sides of my family are amazing in the kitchen and the talent trickled down to my parents. I come from a family of immigrants so a lot of our meals still tie in closely to our heritage. My mom emigrated from Cuba when she was four; my paternal grandfather and grandmother came to America from England and Ireland, respectively. It was not an unusual thing to have *arroz con pollo* one night, corn beef and cabbage the next, and then roast beef and Yorkshire pudding for the following dinner.

Other references are rich in cultural values, such as the following excerpt:

> The next item in my bag is a dollar bill that symbolizes hard work. Many Hispanics are not born into wealth but work very hard for every cent they earn. Many of my ancestors and even living family members work in extreme heat and for long, rigorous hours. Although society often looks down on the lower and middle class Hispanic groups, they have the pride of knowing that they are earning their living and gradually increasing in wealth for the future generation of young Hispanics. Hard work is extremely important in the Hispanic culture; without it, poverty would prevail and change would not come as quickly.

Students often comment that this exercise is one of their favorite and most inspiring course activities:

> I really appreciated this exercise because it helped me to analyze the things in my life that shape who I am. Before I started "My Life in a Bag" I never realized what a huge contribution my culture had on the way I live my life and the decisions I make. I feel a great sense of pride for the things I included in my "My Life in a Bag," and I feel empowered by all of them because I know how influential they are to me.

"My Life in a Bag" is an effective activity to increase pre-service secondary teachers' multicultural awareness, sensitivity, and understanding of the influence of culture on identity. This important insight may assist these aspiring new teachers in using and designing relevant activities through the utilization of their own students as a rich multicultural resource. In summary, I have found "My Life in a Bag" to be a rich, rewarding, and insight-producing activity for educators and students alike.

References

Caruso, J. (1999). My life in a bag. *Electronic Magazine of Multicultural Education 1*(4), 2 paragraphs. Retrieved June 17, 2008, from http://www.eastern.edu/publications/emme/1999fall/caruso.html

National Council for Accreditation of Teacher Education (2008). *Professional standards for the accreditation of teacher preparation institutions.* Retrieved June 17, 2008, from http://www.ncate.org/institutions/standards.asp?ch=8

Pai, Y., Adler, S.A., & Shadiow, L.K. (2006). *Cultural foundations of education.* Upper Saddle River, NJ: Pearson Education, Inc.

Kathryn S. Lee
Texas State University-San Marcos

Team Teaching and Its Effect on Understanding Measurement and Evaluation

For the last two years Dr. Elliot Sharpe and I have been team teaching in a graduate nursing course, Measurement and Evaluation. When this course was developed, it was determined by the Dean of the School of Education that the course should be team taught by a professor in the School of Education and a professor in the School of Health Professions. The goal of this approach was to allow students a broader range of educational experience in relation to primary, secondary, and higher education and its congruence with nursing. In the Spring of 2007 I decided to study my teaching and the team taught approach to determine its effectiveness in understanding measurement and evaluation in the nursing education graduate program. The purpose of the study was to determine what influence team teaching has on the development of teaching strategies in the graduate nursing student. In this course we utilize interactive and participant observer team teaching approaches (Helms, Alvis, and Willis 2005). The study of my teaching allowed me to gather qualitative and quantitative information on the team taught approach and the related effect it had on the development of teaching strategies in the education of nursing students. One aspect of course development which is important to Dr. Sharpe and me is the working backwards approach. We utilize this approach in our teaching and have taught it to our students. It is important for the nurse educator to develop the tools for student evaluation prior to the development of the course content. Students who have used this approach have commented on how well it worked in their course development and obtaining the objectives set forth for the class. One student stated it provided her with insight into her teaching.

The development of this action research study was twofold. The first factor that provided evidence of the need for this study was the lack of literature that addresses the effect team teaching has on the development of a nurse educator and the lack of development of innovative team teaching strategies that assist in role modeling young nurse educators in the development of their role in nursing education. The implementation of a team teaching approach in nursing education provides the student with innovative teaching strategies that enhance learning. The use of team teaching requires commitment from the faculty to stimulate the learning environment. According to the literature team teaching or a collaborative approach to teaching is effective when the faculty members are acquainted with each other's teaching style and maintain open channels of communication (Letterman & Dugan 2004). One factor that increased the effectiveness and reception of the students was the fact that a similar course taught by the education professor was taken by the nursing professor. This provided both professors with insight into the teaching environment prior to engaging in the team teaching experience. Thus, the process of taking classes from the education professor and observing the role modeling of the measurement class enhanced the synergy of the classroom environment with the team taught approach.

The overall impressions of the team taught class revealed that the camaraderie between the two instructors provided the students with a wider range of perspectives on education and clinical aspects of nursing. The students felt the two instructors provided greater clarity in the content areas of the course. The content was not limited to examples related solely to measurement and evaluation but many topics in the academic arena. The course dealt heavily with test construction, and the students stated the examples from education enhanced their understanding of test construction in nursing. They felt their experience in team teaching will be applied best in their practice when they teach in a clinical laboratory setting in nursing education. The graduate students also felt that the modeling of team teaching enhanced their learning and stated that in nursing we always utilize other people to enhance teaching. This approach widens understanding and expands the breadth of knowledge in nursing. A major disadvantage noted by the students was the guidelines for assignments. The students stated they were given the opportunity to think out of the box and they really prefer more stringent guidelines for the assignments. Another disadvantage noted by the students was that two classes were taught individually and not in the team approach. The students stated they felt content was missed due to the lack of teaming. They commented that they did not like tag teaching and preferred the participative approach.

The quantitative results of this study revealed a score of 4.6 on a Likert scale that the students' educational experience was stimulated by the team taught approach. The implementation of a team taught approach increased the students' knowledge base of the subject 4.7 out of 5.0. The results revealed that their interest in the subject was enhanced by both instructors 4.6/5.0. They stated their desire to implement the team taught approach in education of nursing students 4.6/5.0. In conclusion, the team taught approach to nursing education has been both a positive experience for the students and the professors who have undertaken this endeavor.

References

Alvis, J. M., Willis, M., & Helms, M. M. (2005).Planning and implementing shared teaching: An MBA team teaching case study. *Journal of Education for Business* September/October.

Shafer, I. (2001). *Team teaching: Education for the future.* Retrieved March 7, 2007, From the University of Science and Arts of Oklahoma Web Site: http://www.usao.edu/~facshaferi/teamteaching.htm.

Geralyn Frandsen
Maryville University

Classroom Application Strategy: Combining Concept Mapping and Case Studies

An important teaching strategy, concept maps, although not new to nursing, has been utilized to help associate degree nursing (ADN) students learn medical surgical nursing in a new and active way. The strategy enables students to visualize content so comparison and contrast between illnesses can be made. The large wall concept maps, after construction, are used to enhance the student's understanding during case study discussion and application. The purpose is two-fold—the students participate actively, and the content is presented without lecture, saving time to use the class period for case study application exercises.

The concept maps are generated using preprinted, precut terms in size 96 font. The terms include risk factors, assessment data including clinical manifestations and laboratory results, treatments, nursing diagnoses, interventions, and implications. Illness headings are taped to the walls in the classroom. After students are assembled in the classroom, each student is given a packet of randomly shuffled terms. The number of terms (usually seven or eight) in a packet is influenced by how many students are in the class and the number of illnesses being discussed in the class period. The terms are randomly assorted, which means the students actively sort and problem solve as to where the terms fit within the illness diagnoses. The terms are taped onto the wall. Two students are assigned as "experts" for each illness and may utilize their text if needed. The experts monitor the concept map for erroneous information. They can also assist the students with problem solving of where terms may belong. The class is given 10-15 minutes to assemble these large concept maps.

After assembly, a short discussion of each illness and concept map follows. The experts lead this discussion with focusing from the professor. Students are given the opportunity to add any additional information to the concept maps with blank paper. Nursing diagnoses may be the same for many of the illnesses. Nursing actions, rationales and evaluation criteria for each illness are discussed while comparing and contrasting the similarities and differences. The discussion is kept brief since the next step is using the concept maps to apply the information while using a case study.

The next step involves using case studies to emphasize nursing process and care. Focus on expected outcomes and potential complications occur during the case study. Initially, one case study is modeled for the whole group. Small groups (3-4 students) are assigned particular cases to work through for a specific period of time while using the information on the wall to assist them with details and concepts. After the allotted period of time the students come back together and report on their cases. This step allows the other students to take notes on cases they may not have discussed in their small groups and to contribute any additional information or thoughts.

The combination of concept maps and case studies within a class setting enables the students to actively participate and problem solve. The students visualize the information and make connections while using the information in the application. The students are engaged with the material in a learner centered environment. The formation of concept maps allows for minimal to no lecture while still presenting the material. The freedom from using lecture allows time for more application practice using case studies in a content-laden course.

This strategy has been used with second year ADN students in both the first and second semester in the following medical surgical courses—Life Transitions IV: Promotion of Health and Self-Care in Individuals and Families During Later Life and Clinical Decision Making: Models for Nursing Practice. After implementation of the strategy the students' comments included: "the concept maps helped me during tests because I was able to visualize and use the information," "this is a great way to get us to interact and pick each other's brains" and "having to put the maps together in the right order made us use our heads, then putting the information to use with the case studies made us think more like nurses."

Debbie Beyer
Miami University-Hamilton

Scholarship of Teaching and Learning in a Teaching Classroom

"Education is not filling a bucket but lighting a fire."
-William Butler

Good teaching blurs the line between teachers and students; as such, we become eager voyagers on a journey of understanding. Teaching graduate students *how to teach* provides a unique opportunity for a rich exploration of the Boyer's scholarship of teaching. Students are able to participate in this learning journey on many levels: by teaching an undergraduate course themselves under tutelage; by engaging in activities that lend themselves to understanding good teaching; by guest lecturing and receiving extensive feedback about their teaching; and by exploring, like a scientist in a laboratory, why a course is built as it is. Students are initially petrified of teaching, as we once were, and helping them see teaching as a developmental progression instead of a finished, polished act is a helpful framework for them. The following quote from the Teaching of Psychology (TOP) syllabus helps set the stage:

> **Teaching of Psychology (TOP)** is designed to be the class I most wish I had in graduate school. After learning copious amounts about psychology but nothing about teaching, I realized that I was horrifically ill equipped to do what was required of me for approximately 80% of my workdays (I was capable, however, of engaging in the other 20% of my time demands: attending boring meetings). I wish I had read the research on how to design a good course and interact with students in a meaningful way around content information. I also wish I had practiced teaching prior to actually doing it, when I had to get over my paralyzing fears of standing up in front of others and talking. I am sure the students wondered as much as I did where I was going next in my teaching and why. Somehow, I made it through, as will you, but the truth is that I made it up as I went along.

In our TOP course, students report the following activities were the most meaningful to them in strengthening their understanding of the scholarship of teaching and learning:

- Videotape review of students' teaching in undergraduate classes (either classes they are co-teaching or classes in which they guest lecture): as we review videotapes, we stop the tape frequently and comment on what is and is not working about their teaching. We also discuss what directions students-teachers should take next (e.g., "If you were teaching the class on tape, how would you salvage the activity gone awry?")

- Panel of experts: we invite some of the "best teachers" from our university to an informal panel discussion, where the TOP students ask questions, including challenging ones such as "What was your biggest teaching mistake?" and "What do you wish you would have known about teaching as a first year teacher?"

- Teaching portfolio: students create their own teaching portfolios in the class, determining what components the portfolio will include and when it will be due. Components of the portfolio may include learning logs, teaching logs, statements of their teaching philosophy, their reflections on student evaluations, written critiques of a peer's teaching, or completed proposals to present at teaching conferences.

- Exploration of the workings of the TOP course: midterm student feedback is anonymously collected (what is/is not working in this course), typewritten, and shared with the class, who then have an opportunity to reflect on the feedback and discuss how we best understand it and what we should change as we critically reflect on it.

- "Front of the room" activities: students initially practice just being in front of the room, then practice telling a story, then sharing a joke, then teaching something they learned about teaching from one of the classic books we are reading about teaching.

- Role plays: students role play managing difficult students, including monologuers, nodders (sleepy students), wallflowers, challengers, brown-nosers, soap-boxers, chit-chatters, and likeable-but-not-so-bright students. In this safe context, TOP students can experiment with different techniques to manage some of the more difficult students they might encounter.

- Teaching role model: students embark on a reflective journey and write about their best teachers, and then they return to the classroom to discuss the gifts of this teacher and how they themselves can evidence some of these ideals in their own teaching.

- Learner-centered continuum: we draw a continuum on the board to illustrate a spectrum of teaching philosophies, ranging from learner-centered at one end point to teacher-centered on the other. Students have a set of post-it notes on which they write specific classes they have taken, and then they place these notes where they feel they "fit" along the continuum. We then discuss what makes classes learner-centered, and if/how classes can be "good" classes but not learner-centered, using their specific examples as anchors for this discussion.

- Honest in-the-moment, process conversations: these dialogs allow students to see how teachers think and spontaneously shift activities ("I sensed that collectively you were getting bored and were ready to move on to a new activity; was I mistaken? How did I know this?"). These activities allow for students to see "the hot dog being made," as it were, by helping them understand the microskills involved in good teaching.
- Problem-based learning around grading: I share my fears and frustrations around assigning grades and note that grading has always felt disconnected from learning, judgmental, and arbitrary to me, and I ask students to explore this "real world" problem, analyze it, and explore possible solutions.

Students note the most useful activities from this list include class review and feedback of their teaching videotapes, role-playing difficult students, and the live supervision provided when they are teaching. Good teaching, it turns out, can be taught, especially if we heed Boyer's call to consider the Scholarship of Teaching in our work and approach our teaching in a thoughtful, critically reflective way.

DeDe Wohlfarth
Beth Simon
Dan Sheras
Jody Pimentel
Laura Gabel
Jess Bennett
Spalding University

Using SWEAT Pages to Engage Students with Text

Surfing the Net has added "efficiency" and "immediacy" to what we read, but faculty want students to be more than "decoders of information." Faculty want students to read deeply, make connections, read without distractions, and become engaged with text material.

SWEAT pages [See attachment] provide students a one-page format for interacting with written materials, allowing them to "make the material their own."

The SWEAT page consists of three parts:

QUESTIONS: The top part of the page provides lines on which students write questions based on Bloom's Taxonomy—going from low-level (knowledge, comprehension, application) to higher-level (analysis, synthesis, evaluation). These questions can be generated before, during or after the student has read the entire text. Students typically write from 5-7 questions; as the semester progresses, these questions move from lower-level to higher-level, more complex questions.

GRAPHIC: The second section/middle part of the page is a box. Here the student creates a graph, sketch, concept map, or other visual of the text material. The brain is a pattern-seeking device and absorbs pictures more easily than text; the visual helps transfer information into long-term memory. Instructors can "see at a glance" the level of comprehension and connections which the student has formed from the reading. Visual learners *love* this part of the SWEAT page.

SUMMARY: The third part of the page provides lines on which students write a concise summary of the text information. This summary should be no more that 3-4 sentences. Summarizing material identifies the most important information, identifies/creates a thesis statement, puts the material in the student's own language, and helps the brain consolidate the information.

There are many advantages of Teaching Using SWEAT Pages:
- Gives Teaching/Learning an Immediate Foundation
- Shows Tangible "Proof" of Reading the Assignment
- Shows Material as a Visual (Graphic, Concept Map, Timeline, etc.)
- Shows Student "Grasp" of Main Idea of the Reading
- Gives Student Practice in Summary Skills
- Gives Students "Ownership" of Material by Putting It In Their Own Words (Paraphrase)
- Provides Student Practice in Paraphrasing
- Organizes Student Thought About the Reading
- Forces Student to Work Through "Muddy Thinking"
- Shows Analytical Thinking
- Allows Student to Access Prior Knowledge
- Allows Student to Create Questions at ALL Levels of Bloom's Taxonomy
- Works as a Presentation Tool
- Works as a Study Tool
- Organizes Study Groups
- Works as a Review Tool
- Addresses ALL Levels of Bloom's Taxonomy: Knowledge, Application, Analysis, Synthesis and—If "Critique" is Added—Also Covers Evaluation

- Keeps Students "On Task"
- Allows Instructors to "See at a Glance" Student Comprehension Levels of the Reading Material

I have incorporated SWEAT pages into all of my first-year courses—College Reading Methods, College Critical Reading, Study Skills, and FSU Seminars. Once the students have been taught and practiced the SWEAT page format, it becomes "second nature" to them. Once mastered, students consistently say SWEAT pages are their "best reading strategy."

As Maryanne Wolf says, "We are not only *what* we read," but "we are how we read." SWEAT pages give students a framework they can internalize, they can utilize in their other academic courses, and they can take with them on their life-long reading journey.

Helen E. Woodman
Ferris State University

_____

Sweat Page

Questions:

_____
_____
_____
_____
_____
_____
_____
_____
_____
_____
_____
_____
_____

Graphic:

Summary:

_____
_____
_____
_____
_____
_____
_____
_____
_____
_____

Within the Criminal Justice Classroom

Applying knowledge learned within the classroom to the CSI generation helps better educate students on the reality of life in a later career.

Criminal justice students come into the classroom expecting to learn about and become what they see on television. They all want to be CSI agents and to research serial killers. Little do they know that there are not enough serial killers in history for them each to study a different one and crime is rarely, if ever, solved in an hour. These preconceived notions are rigid, deep set, and difficult to change. Using the following five techniques of application aids faculty in breaking those barriers:

1. Bring in a guest speaker who is currently working in the field to explain how the knowledge learned in the classroom applies to the decisions they make everyday in the field. For online courses, ask the guest speaker to chat live with your students.
2. Have students interview a police/courts/or corrections officer in person on how their jobs compare and contrast to what is portrayed in the media or what is disseminated through course materials.
3. Provide an opportunity for extra credit if students ride along with a police officer, sit in the courtroom to watch an active docket for a certain time frame, or spend the day in a correctional facility. Ask them to present their experience to the class and tell the class how the experience compared to what they learned in the book or within your classroom.
4. Have students present a section of the book to the class and ask them to include what questions they had or topics they were interested in that were *not* covered in the book. Students in the class can then engage in discussions and the faculty member can direct the conversation as he or she deem appropriate.
5. Provide a case study scenario to the students. Use an interactive CD (often provided by book publishers), a small group activity, or a case study that you have created to engage students in role-playing. For example, set up a crime scene and discuss jurisdiction, warrants, and process [from the standpoint of the police (process), courts (judgment), and corrections (punitive sanctioning)].

These techniques have proven to be highly successful in the Introduction to Criminal Justice Course that I have taught. Students become engaged with the material, begin working better with each other, feel more comfortable speaking out in class, and are able to apply book learning to numerous aspects of their future careers. They often comment on course evaluations how much they enjoyed the "Application Activities." These techniques may also be utilized in other courses, disciplines, and course formats (traditional, hybrid, or online) with simple modifications.

Alana Van Gundy–Yoder
Miami University Hamilton

_____

Why Do I Have to Take This Class?

Integrating information into your course from different academic disciplines results in a better sense of connectedness for students.

Boyer's concept of integration focuses on giving meaning to isolated facts through the connection of knowledge, context, and perspective. There is no better way to do this then by showing how your discipline affects, or is affected by other disciplines. I make it a point to place the material I cover in my class within the context of other disciplines so that students can understand inter-connectedness of their courses. With the increasing global market and the emphasis in my courses on the systems approach, this approach allows students to better answer the question, "Why do I have to take this class?"

While teaching Criminal Justice to introductory students, I try to engage them in activities, discussions and assignments that focus on the effect that the criminal justice system has on: Economics, Political Science, Sociology, Criminology, Psychology, and even History. Similarly, I also ask them to look at how these systems affect criminal justice. A brief example of how this connection may be possible is by examining Sociology. I provide my students with the definition of Criminal Justice and the definition of Sociology, and I literally place the definitions side by side on a Power Point slide or on two index cards. We then dissect the definitions, find commonalities, and dissimilarities between the two subjects. Then I discuss how crime is related to human behavior (the sociological perspective). How might victimization make one act in public? How might being an offender make you change your behavior around pro-social people?

Another way of integrating cross-disciplinary material into a course is utilizing a checklist or a table. Place your discipline on one side of the column/checklist and the outside discipline you are contrasting with on the other side (this example will utilize components of Political Science). Then have students check off or draw arrows between the concepts they feel are related. I guarantee this process will cause students to start looking "outside the box," and it proves to be a stimulus for rather fruitful conversation. The activity that you provide to the students may look like this (for the sake of space this is a very simple table, but it can obviously be made more complicated):

Activity One:

The purpose of this activity is for you to look at how Criminal Justice is related to other academic disciplines. Look at the table below and think for a moment about what sort of relationships each word (concept) has with the others. Please follow the remaining instructions, and we will discuss your answers tonight in class.

First, think about what type of a relationship might exist between the concepts on each side of the table. If you feel that a relationship exists where one concept affects another, but there is no reciprocal relationship (for example the structure of criminal justice affects the government, but the government does not affect the structure of criminal justice) draw a single-headed arrow (→) **from the concept that you feel affects the other one to the one you feel is affected.** If you think that a relationship exists where both concepts affect each other, please draw a double-headed arrow (↔).

Criminal Justice	Political Science
Structure	Government
Management	Laws/Legislatures
Employment	Funding
Police	Elections
Courts	Policy Creation
Corrections	Political Correctness

Next, choose one concept that you have given a single-headed arrow, and explain to me why you responded in that manner.

_____
_____
_____

Choose one concept that you have given a double-headed arrow, and explain to me why you responded in that manner.

_____
_____
_____

Lastly, what does this exercise tell you about the integration of concepts between Criminal Justice and Political Science?

_____

_____

_____

This activity has been very successful in my Introduction to Criminal Justice course as well as my Sociology courses. Students begin to see why the course is important as well as why they need to integrate or connect concepts to other parts of their life. They begin to think outside of the box, and oftentimes they come up to me after class and tell me that they now understand the meaning of "putting something in perspective."

Alana Van Gundy - Yoder
Miami University Hamilton

_____

Senior Research: Scholarship – Discovered, Integrated, Applied, and Taught

A scholar is both "a learned or erudite person, one who has profound knowledge of a particular subject" and "a student or pupil." Boyer's articulation of four distinctive types of scholarship includes both aspects of scholarship contained in the definition of scholars as those who are simultaneously both teachers and learners. What we teach and learn in any discipline is framed by the knowledge and professional practice of our discipline. Each of Boyer's four types of scholarship has important implications for the design of any course, but this is especially true for those intended to provide students with a scholarship capstone.

Empiricism, the use of observation and evidence to develop an integrated and coherent body of knowledge, is a process at the heart of all science. The scientific method embodies the essence of empiricism; it is an interdependent and ultimately self-correcting set of activities that has evolved to allow scientists to disprove themselves. This notion of falsifiability is the single characteristic which most clearly distinguishes the sciences from other disciplines. The goal of science programs, including those in the social sciences, should be to encourage students to learn to think scientifically as well as to master a body of knowledge associated with their respective discipline. As the Roman historian Plutarch so famously observed, "The mind is not a vessel to be filled, but a fire to be kindled." Boyer's four types of scholarship help realize this goal.

The psychology major at Berea College includes a capstone course in senior research (PSY 424). In this course each student is expected to design, conduct and analyze a psychological experiment and present the result in a 15 minute public presentation, a professional poster, and a 7-10 page research paper. This is a daunting task, a challenge that is unusual at the undergraduate level. Although classes are small at this rural liberal arts college, the 6-12 students who enroll in the course each semester require considerable support and encouragement to produce the kind of work in which they (and the college) can take pride.

Boyer's four types of scholarship provide a framework for considering this course and its recently increased success. This course focuses directly on the scholarship of discovery. All psychology students complete extensive study about the scientific method in previous courses in general psychology, statistics, and research design as well as other elective psychology courses and laboratories. However, as a capstone this particular course seeks to integrate the material from many of the other psychology courses. The capstone course begins with brief reviews of the most critical information about research methods and statistics. The goal is for all students to gain an appreciation for the interconnectedness of the scientific methods and psychology's current body of knowledge. What makes this capstone unique pedagogically is the extent to which students are expected to apply what they have learned to a project of their own making. Finally, by requiring students to report their findings in three different modalities, the course requires each of them to become teachers as they struggle to prioritize, simplify, organize and communicate the story of their own experiment and what they have discovered.

Students have a great deal of freedom in this course. Although daily quizzes taken early in the course are a major portion of their midterm grade, they are not a part of the final grade. There are four mandatory milestones that are graded on a pass-fail basis (a draft proposal, a final proposal, a dummy data analysis, and a mock presentation) each worth 2.5%. The largest single component of each student's final grade is the quality of her or his experiment (40%) with 100% allocated to how well the student was able to present the research in three modes (written, spoken, and graphic). The final 20% of the final grade is devoted to students' own research reflection in which they are asked to integrate their experiences from across the semester.

There are many ways in which such a course might be evaluated. Course critique results show that students report devoting many more hours to this course compared to the campus average. For example, 63% of the students enrolled in the capstone course over the last two years reported spending more than 10 hours/week on the course compared to the 36% of students who reported spending this much time on all other courses. Students also rate the course more than one half standard deviation above the campus average for promoting independent thinking, requiring a high level of performance, having clear objectives, showing concern for student progress, and being graded fairly. Students' self-reports of their knowledge as measured by a knowledge survey of nearly 50 key concepts given both before and after the course show significant gains in most areas. In fact, in over 50% of these areas students express confidence that they could provide clear and complete explanations of these important concepts compared to fewer than 20% of the same concepts when they enter the course. The grade distribution is high, with approximately two thirds of the students earning A's or A-'s. General feedback from other students and faculty members who attend the presentations and see the poster displays attests to the high quality of scholarship. Similarly, publications and competitive awards for student presentations at local and regional research gatherings corroborate the excellence of student research. At the completion of the course, 45% of the students report having learned "an exceptional amount" compared to the campus average of 24% for all other courses. The following conclusion from a student learning reflection is similar to many of those received:

> I worked harder in this course than any other in my college career. I suppose this is how it's supposed to be though - they don't call it 'capstone' for nothing. I learned a lot about myself through the process of designing an experiment that I was interested in and would be committed to.

Dave Porter
Berea College

_____

Blogging: The Nexus of Theory and Practice

Upon retirement in 2003, after 31 years in the public schools, I began teaching educational leadership and educational foundations courses on a few central Kentucky campuses: Eastern Kentucky University, the University of Kentucky, Georgetown College, and Kentucky State University.

It became immediately apparent that most of my graduate students - practicing teachers themselves – were frustrated by the disconnect between their own idealized version of what it meant to be a good teacher and the realities of life under No Child Left Behind. Far too many were simply unable to understand the philosophical shift that occurred when NCLB's accountability system required data disaggregation in a high-stakes/"no excuses" environment. The shift from "Equality of Education Opportunity" to "Equity of Student Achievement Outcomes" left many wondering how they could fairly be held responsible for all student achievement outcomes.

I learned that many of these teachers were relatively removed from the larger policy conversations going on around them, conversations that were impacting their lives.

In order to promote teacher leadership among my students so that they might engage in these important debates, I was challenged to bring together the "foundational material" and the dynamic content of "current events." The foundational material is based along very traditional scholastic lines. But the "current events" portion is not. It is drawn largely from journalistic sources utilizing internet resources.

Good teachers have been using news articles to enhance instruction for a long time now. But today's technology has transformed the scope of what constitutes trustworthy knowledge and has put powerful tools of inquiry into the hands of our students. Countless numbers of reliable sources now exist on the Internet. By directing students to the most credible sources, and teaching them to be skeptical and think for themselves, it is now possible to utilize these tools - without losing control of the curriculum - and preserve scholarly traditions in the process.

To support this effort, I created a blog (Kentucky School News & Commentary http://theprincipal.blogspot.com) where I aggregate state and national school news - with occasional commentary.

This is not a typical blog where one might post personal thoughts and rants. I moderate the blog and insist that all content and comments are written in a professional tone that is free from the kinds of name-calling and personal attacks seen on many blogs. This requirement contributes to the desired tone of my students' written work.

If there is a down-side, it is the amount of time required to produce high quality content. Fortunately, Eastern Kentucky University counts such faculty contributions as "service" for tenure and promotion purposes.

On a weekly basis, I
- Post a number of news stories
- Talk with state and local news-makers
- Write commentary on selected items
- Follow certain "big stories" pertaining to the state board of education, education commissioner and other groups
- Occasionally produce original reporting

On one occasion, original research posted on the blog revealed a number of "resume errors" made by a woman who had just been named education commissioner. The blog stories were picked up by members of the mainstream press, who are regular readers, and eventually led to a decision by the commissioner-elect to resign her position prior to taking office.

Since I maintain the blog, I am able to quickly focus on items that come up in class and provide real-life examples of what's happening in the field, today. For example this afternoon, a student in our special education cohort wanted to know more about the use of aversive techniques at a special education school in Massachusetts. By tomorrow, I will have posted a link to several stories about the school. Kentucky School News & Commentary is easily searchable by keyword and serves as a news repository for students.

The blog's effect has been that students are better able and more willing to engage in classroom debates on topics of immediate interest. It has also proven useful to other professors in their classes. Drs. Steve and June Hyndman of Georgetown College and Eastern Kentucky University respectively use Kentucky School News & Commentary in their technology classes and in other education classes as a web resource. Steve says the blog is "both a one-stop site for education news at the state and national levels and also an excellent example of the effectiveness of blogs as education and communication tools." June likes the way the issues are "thoroughly investigated and all points of view are honored. Richard offers a 'level-headed' analysis of the most important of education issues."

After 18 months, the blog has gained some unanticipated notoriety, ranking (at the time of this writing) as the 6th most influential political blog in Kentucky according to BlogNetNews.com. News editors, state board of education members, local superintendents, principals, teachers and others who are influential in education policy circles have taken notice.

I would argue that the practice fits Ernest Boyer's broadened vision of scholarship. It contributes to the intellectual climate (discovery) of the university; makes connections across disciplines (integration); is clearly service-oriented and sits at the nexus of theory and practice (application); and at a university whose goals are Teaching, Research and Service (in that order) it models and promotes scholarly teaching for future teachers (teaching).

Richard Day
Eastern Kentucky University

_____

Using Analogy to Teach Primary Sources

One of the most common problems I find when grading undergraduate student term papers is the overuse of secondary sources. It has been very challenging to get students to understand the importance of citing primary scholarly sources when they prepare their bibliographies. For the purposes of this teaching strategy, I use Burton and Chadwick's (2000) definition of primary and secondary sources. While they admit that the terms can vary across disciplines, they use the following description for the hard sciences: "a primary source is the original research. A secondary source summarizes or discusses the primary research" (Burton & Chadwick, 2000, pg. 322). Increasingly, students are submitting bibliographies that list websites, newspaper articles, and Wikipedia entries as if these references represent the original source of information. Sutton and Knight (2006) have studied the issue of teaching students the difference between primary and secondary sources. They point out that there is little research being conducted in the area of primary source instruction. "A review of the professional literature reveals a scarcity of strategies for extending primary source instruction to students in general library classes through an information literacy based pedagogy" (Sutton & Knight, 2006, p.321). The "scarcity of strategies" they mention suggests a need for a practical teaching method. As a professor assigning undergraduate research papers in a broadcast media management course, I decided to prepare an instructional strategy designed to teach students the importance of using primary sources in their term papers. Before I explain this strategy, it is important to point out why students may be having such a difficult time understanding the importance of using primary sources.

Scholars who have studied undergraduate research behavior have said that students choose sources on the basis of convenience and not on the basis of originality (Davis, 2003; Valentine, 2001). Students tend to choose sources that they think are easy to find, easy to understand, and easy to cite. Much of this convenience can be satisfied by the use of Internet sources. During the rise of Internet popularity among college students, Davis (2003) found a significant increase of Internet sources (as opposed to more traditional sources like books and research articles) in student bibliographies. A more recent indicator of this reliance on Internet sources is the growing popularity of online encyclopedia websites like Wikipedia. The Pew Internet and American Life Project (2007) released a report revealing that 36 % of online adults consult Wikipedia. In addition, 50% of these users have a college degree. This search for convenience and this dependence on the Internet for sources are a couple of reasons that students seem to be indifferent to the need to use primary sources in their bibliographies.

I have experienced some isolated cases in which students have shown a blatant disregard for the attribution of credit to researchers for their ideas. An alarming pattern of plagiarism has emerged as a major concern on many college campuses. In his longitudinal study on student cheating, Schab (1991) found that the percentage of students who admitted to copying material word for word out of a book without citing the information increased from 67% in 1969 to 76% in 1989. The problem of plagiarism not only suggests a lack of awareness of the formal rules of citation, but a misguided understanding that citing sources is an insignificant act and there are no negative consequences for stealing another person's idea. Taking this issue into consideration, we shouldn't find it surprising that so many students write term papers without a clear understanding that using primary sources is an important part of determining the credibility of research papers.

Even though many obstacles confronting professors who teach research to undergraduates exist, showing my students the benefits of using primary sources is worthwhile. In her research, Morgan (2002) says that students who read and study primary sources will become more skillful at sorting, analyzing, and synthesizing large amounts of information. D'Aniello (1993) recommends the use of primary sources to students because they learn to emulate the research practice of scholars and they begin to understand the contextual framework of information.

The following teaching strategy contains the use of an analogy to demonstrate the importance of primary sources. Research has shown that incorporating analogies into teaching strategies can enhance student understanding and reduce misconceptions (Glynn, 1991). The instructor begins this procedure by speaking very generally about the need for accuracy in bibliographic sources. Then the instructor facilitates a classroom exercise to engage students and establish the basis for the analogy. In this case, using secondary sources will be presented as analogous to participating in a "whisper-down-the-lane" exercise. At the end of the exercise, the instructor uses the analogy to highlight the inaccuracy of using secondary sources. The following is a summary of how I have conducted this lesson in a broadcast management course:

"Today we are going to talk about the importance of accurate references in your bibliographic sources. In order to demonstrate my point today, I want us to engage in a class exercise. I have a passage from a study that I want to show you. Let's assume that this hypothetical passage contains the conclusions from a journal article that you want to cite in your term paper. In order to reference this passage, you will need to determine what it says accurately. I will show the entire class the passage on one condition. Each person must whisper the passage into the ear of the person sitting next to them." (For this exercise it is worth arranging the seats of the class in a semi circle in order to make it easier for the students to complete the exercise). "Only one person will get to actually look at the passage, and that person will initiate the exercise. Everyone else must depend on the recollection of the person who whispers the passage into their ear. When the exercise is complete, the last person to hear the passage will repeat what they heard out loud and they will write their recollection on the chalk board. I will then reveal the original passage on an overhead so that we can compare the two versions together as a class. (I used the following hypothetical passage in a broadcast management class of only 6 students on the junior or senior level.)

Original Passage: This study finds that media employees showed evidence of increased production when managers gave consistent and frequent feedback.
(I allowed one student to read and closely examine the passage until she felt comfortable with her recollection. She than initiated the exercise. Students were not allowed to write anything down, and they were only permitted to whisper. This restriction makes each student depend on a summarized or paraphrased version of the original. This is how the exercise parallels the reliance on secondary sources. After the class completed the exercise, the last student wrote down his recollection on the chalk board).

Student's Recollection: Managers found evidence of increased production when their workers gave consistent feedback.

(At this point, the instructor facilitates a classroom discussion designed to point out the inaccuracy of the student version. These questions could help toward that end.) "Would you feel comfortable citing the student recollection in your research paper?" "Does this recollection accurately reflect the original version?" (After the discussion, I would clarify the analogy to the entire class by saying something to the following effect.) "Think back during the exercise. Notice that every time someone whispered the passage into the ear of one of their classmates, a new layer of sourcing was created. Each layer represented a version that was further removed from the original source. In this case the primary source was represented by the original passage – or the researchers who conducted the original study. The person who started off the exercise became the secondary source. The third person became the tertiary source and so on. Notice the further we got from the primary source, the more inaccurate the information became. This is why it is so important to find the original sources in your term papers!" (At this point, I show some specific examples of secondary source citations from old term papers that previous students submitted – without revealing their identity. I end the session with a strong caution to the students about using websites that depend on secondary sources for their documentation.)

This teaching strategy will reach some students, but it will not be a cure-all. Some students will still need more clarification of primary and secondary sourcing. Specifically, I've found this exercise to be effective at generating more engaged student learning about research. This strategy tends to make students more active in asking questions about the sources they are using in their papers.

References

Burton, V.T., & Chadwick, S.A. (2000). Investigating the practices of student researchers: Patterns of use and criteria for use of internet and library sources. *Computers and Composition 17* (3), 309-328.

D'Aniello, C.A. (1993). Bibliographic instruction in history. In C.A. D'Aniello (Ed.), *Teaching bibliographic skills in history: A sourcebook for historians and librarians* (pp. 69-93). Westport CT: Greenwood Press.

Davis, P.M. (2003). Effect of the web on undergraduate citation behavior: Guiding student scholarship in the networked age. *Portal: Libraries and the Academy 3*(1), 41-51.

Glynn, S. (1991). Explaining science concepts: A teaching with analogies model. In S. Glynn, R. Yeany & B. Britton (Eds.), *The Psychology of Learning Science* (pp. 219-240). Hillsdale, NJ: Lawrence Erlbaum.

Morgan, K.R. (2002). Using primary sources to build a community of thinkers. *English Journal 91*, 69-74.

Pew Internet & American Life Project. (2007, April 24). *36% of online American adults consult wikipedia.* Retrieved June 28, 2008 from http://www.pewinternet.org/PPF/r/212/report_display.asp.

Schab, F. (1991). Schooling without learning: Thirty years of cheating in high school. *Adolescence 23*, 839-847.

Sutton, S., & Knight, L. (2006). Beyond the reading room: Integrating primary and secondary sources in the library classroom. *The Journal of Academic Librarianship 32* (3), 320-325.

Valentine, B. (2001). The legitimate effort in research papers: Student commitment vs. faculty expectations. *The Journal of Academic Librarianship 27* (2), 107-115.

Eric K. Jones
Otterbein College

Fostering Collaborations

Strategies to Enhance Scholarship and Mentoring in Faculty Student Research

As professionals in higher education, we see clearly the advantages of including undergraduate students in research and scholarly activities. Numerous studies have reported the benefits of utilizing undergraduate student researchers and the positive outcomes of such collaborations: helping learners further hone their thinking and research skills, clarifying and confirming career paths, and further enhancing their interest in, and preparation for, graduate school (Hathaway, Nagda, & Gregerman, 2002; Seymour, E. et. al., 2004; Cremer & Bringle, 1990). While the student benefit is profound, faculty have also experienced positive outcomes in their ability to tackle more complex research questions and use limited resources in a more efficient manner, in addition to expanding ways they connect with their students. Yet in the presence of such uplifting research, it is equally important to consider the challenges and create strategies to address and to possibly avoid the pitfalls of collaborative research, including authorship order and workload distribution (Bennett & Kidwell, 2001; Hathaway, Nagda, & Gregerman, 2002; Goodyear, Crego & Johnston, 1992)

This concern leads us to the ethical imperative of creating mutually beneficial scholarly collaborations, partnerships between faculty and student that provide mentoring throughout the research process and contribute to a foundation of knowledge. A Student-Faculty Research Agreement helps to formalize the terms of research collaborations between students and their mentor for a designated project. A Student-Faculty Research Agreement addresses specific tasks, responsibilities, issues related to the conduct of scientific research (such as authorship, research ethics, ownership of information/ideas, etc.). Such an agreement is highly generalizable and can be used in any undergraduate or graduate level course, research project, honors project, thesis advising, or even as a template for collaborative research with colleagues.

Examples of a Student-Faculty Research Agreement we found most helpful include the following links:

http://facpub.stjohns.edu/~roigm/research%20contract.html

http://www.ugresearch.umd.edu/programs/agreement.pdf

http://edweb6.educ.msu.edu/kin/BylawsPolicies/Research.pdf

Many benefits exist for both students and faculty who participate in collaborative research endeavors. We recommend a review of examples of projects within your discipline and urge you to consider ways to involve undergraduates in your scholarly efforts. As you ponder such scholarly collaborations, consider utilizing a Student-Faculty Research Agreement to ensure a mutually beneficial scholarly experience for all.

Amber Dailey-Hebert
Emily Donnelli-Sallee
B. Jean Mandernach
Park University

Turning Independent Study Opportunities into Student/Faculty Presentations and Publications

One of the experiences that I have learned can be truly rewarding for a university professor is mentoring a student through an independent study. Although many faculty avoid supervising independent studies because of the extra (often unpaid and unappreciated) work it involves to supervise the student in such study, I have had a number of successful independent studies where the final product was a student-delivered presentation at a professional conference or a peer-reviewed publication (with several more currently waiting for me to do my part to finalize them for publication as well). Here is the approach that I use.

First, and foremost, at the beginning of the semester, in each class that I teach I mention at the end of the second day of class that if there are any students who want to get their "feet wet" with research, I would be happy to talk to them about independent study opportunities. Because most students (especially at the undergraduate level) have no idea what an independent study consists of, and most student at the universities where I have taught have full-time jobs or have other time-consuming obligations outside of class, there are never many students who are interested. I have found, however, that those who approach me after that announcement are almost always serious students with a strong work ethic who have some confidence in their writing and research abilities. As such, this method allows me to be somewhat selective in the students I choose to work with (as opposed to the independent studies where I am asked to deliver a course because the student "couldn't fit it into their schedule," "needs to graduate this semester and the course isn't offered again for a year," etc.). In the latter situations, from my experience, it is almost always counterproductive to collaborate on a research project in lieu of (or in addition to) the material required to be covered for that course. As such, I offer my first caveat: if you cannot establish the parameters for the course delivery and product, but still choose to supervise an independent study, view the experience as service to the student and your department. Do a good job, make sure the student learns the required content, but do not try to turn that independent study into a conference presentation or peer-reviewed publication unless you are willing to do the majority of the work to complete the project.

After recruiting interested students, I then give the student several options. I am fortunate in that I have access to data from a wide variety of settings; as such, I almost always have data that can easily be turned into a publishable product. Consequently students, have some choice in their research topic (which makes them far more vested in the project); this arrangement has invariably led to a situation where the student and I created a worthwhile presentation or publication. After the student selects the topic in which he or she is most interested, we then move to the next phase of the relationship: the independent study contract.

The contract (and its enforcement) is probably the most important part of distinguishing an independent study where the faculty works hard with little or no reward from the independent study where the faculty and student produce a product that is presentable or publishable. The typical contract I create has four key parts:

1. A timeline for completion of the project, with pieces of the project due at various dates throughout the semester;
2. A requirement that the student meet with me at either weekly or bi-monthly intervals;
3. A requirement that the student have a final product (whether it be a conference presentation or a paper to be submitted to a journal) completed by the end of the semester **and a date by which that product must be submitted to me**; and
4. A clause that states the only reason for an Incomplete grade in this course is either (a) serious medical illness or (b) military service. Both of these situations must directly involve the student, not a close family member or friend.

After creating the contract, I typically ask the student to look the contract over and sign it if amenable to the cooperative project. I ask the student to pay particular attention to the second and last points, as they are the two most difficult parts of the contract for most students. Below I discuss each component of the contract in greater detail.

A timeline for completion of the project -- This portion of the contract informs the student of both the scope and the nature of the work he or she will have to accomplish during the semester. More experienced students often view an independent study as a "gravy course" (and, in reality, many are). As such, this part of the contract lets the student know that this particular independent study is not one of those courses.

A requirement that the student meet with me at either weekly or bi-monthly intervals –Honestly, this portion of the contract is more for me than for the student. Because I always have a number of projects going on at any time, this regular meeting gives me both focus and deadlines so that I can uphold my part of the independent study collaboration, whatever that may be. My experience has also been that students are a lot like me; if we do not have regularly scheduled meetings with products due at those meetings, they often procrastinate until it is too late to submit a quality product. These meetings thus hold both me and the student to a greater level of accountability.

A requirement that the student have a final product completed by the end of the semester – This is often the most difficult portion of the contract for the student to complete and for me to enforce. Nevertheless, I have found that when I agree to the independent study at the beginning of the semester and discuss this particular requirement with the student up-front, I feel far better assigning a C, D, or F when needed. Furthermore, the student rarely complains because he or she realizes the failure to complete the project was his or her responsibility, not mine. Fortunately, since I have begun using this contract idea, I have had this experience only a limited number of times.

A clause that limits the assignment of an Incomplete grade – This is perhaps the most important component of the contract because, in reality, an assignment of an Incomplete grade often signals an (a) uncompleted project and (b) a failed independent study for the student. Neither of those situations is productive; as such, I let the student know from the outset of the project that he or she must complete the project by the end of the semester. Although I have no empirical evidence to support this argument, I think this part of the contract makes the independent study project one that is constantly on the mind of the student throughout the semester. As such, students are far less likely to procrastinate and not complete the project.

Upon the student signing the contract, we then begin to work immediately on the project for which we agreed to collaborate. In my career, the primary projects that have successfully turned into presentations or publications involved students helping me with (a) literature reviews for projects for which I already had data but no time to conduct the literature review or (b) data collection for projects where I had the need for local or regional data.

Below I have listed four publications that are products where students were involved in independent studies as part of the publication process. Each is discussed in some detail below the citation.

Lowe, Nathan, David C. May, & Preston Elrod (2008). Theoretical Predictors of Delinquency among Public School Students in Kentucky: The Roles of Context and Gender. Forthcoming in *Youth Violence and Juvenile Justice.*

> This publication involved a student who approached me and asked if I could teach him structural equation modeling as an independent study. I did so, and we analyzed data that a colleague and I had collected to create an article that will appear in print in 2008.

Williams, Alisha, David C. May, and Peter B. Wood (2008). The Lesser of Two Evils? A Qualitative Study of Offenders' Preferences for Prison Compared to Alternatives. *Journal of Offender Rehabilitation, 46*(3,4), 71-90.

> This publication involved the student going through a number of transcripts of interviews that we had previously conducted, making sense of those interviews, then collaborating with me to create a qualitative paper around the nature of those interviews.

Mustard, Sarah, David C. May, and Daniel Phillips (2006). Prevalence and Predictors of Cheating on Antabuse: Is Antabuse a Cure or Merely an Obstacle? American Journal of Criminal Justice, 31(1), 51-63.

> In this publication, the student and I spent two days interviewing respondents outside a clinic where patients were court-ordered to take Antabuse (a drug that makes individuals violently ill when they drink alcohol) as part of their sanction. We both collected the data, she entered it, the three of us collaborated on the literature review, and we created a truly unique publication that provides a perspective that had previously been ignored in the literature.

May, David C., Peter Wood, Jennifer Mooney, & Kevin Minor (2005). Predicting Offender-Generated Exchange Rates: Implications for a Theory of Sentence Severity. *Crime and Delinquency, 51*(3), 373-399.

> In this publication, the student assisted me with data collection by visiting probation/parole offices and interviewing probationers and parolees at those offices. Although the student did not help much with the eventual publication, we all felt that she had done enough to warrant authorship on the eventual product.

As you can see, the types of activities in which the students were involved vary greatly, but generally involved data collection or analysis (although I have worked on a number of presentations where the students were largely responsible for the literature review portion of the project).

In every one of the aforementioned situations, the students had both a great learning experience and a product that they can be proud of for the rest of their lives. Nevertheless, I would argue that I received far more reward from the collaborations than any of those students. While having an article accepted for publication no longer brings the sheer excitement and joy that it did earlier in my career, the tremor and excitement I see and hear in student's actions and voices when they find out that they are being published makes every hour I spent on the project time well-spent. While I rarely have a student in the traditional classroom thank me (sometimes through tears) for helping them learn and produce, it has happened more than once at the culmination of an independent study project. It is those rare moments that make me remember why I chose this profession and why I continue to do what I do for students at the university.

David C. May
Eastern Kentucky University

Preventing "Author Disorder": The Ethics of Coauthored Publications With Students

When I first saw the request for contributions for this book, I emailed the editors about several topics that might be appropriate as subjects to include in a publication such as this one. Almost as an aside, I asked them what they thought of another idea. The text of that portion of the email is included verbatim below:

> I also have an axe to grind with many of my colleagues, and this might be a good forum for it. The topic would be something like "Is it ever acceptable for faculty to be first author on a publication where they use a student paper" or something like that. The point would be that there are a lot of faculty who use their students as slaves, have them do the lion's share of the work on a paper, then take the paper, list themselves as first author and the student as second author, then submit the article for publication. In my mind, this procedure is not only unethical, it is immoral, but I know some people don't share that opinion. Is this a good place for that?

I include that text to let you know that I find it difficult to be completely objective on this topic. In this article, I will discuss the causes and consequences of what I will call "author disorder." In my mind, author disorder occurs when the order of authorship on the final product that appears in print does not match the amount of contribution of the authors who wrote the article. For this particular discussion, then, author disorder occurs when Student A does the majority of the work for a project on which he or she is collaborating with Faculty Member B. When the product appears in print, however,

Faculty Member B is listed as the lead author followed by Student A.

Many faculty members fall into the trap of author disorder because of the nature of the university professor occupation. After receiving the first tenure-track position, they immediately begin a five- to seven-year-period where, for many, all aspects of their life revolve around the number, type, and order of authorship for papers that they write. This pressure, as well as the subsequent pressure to be promoted after a faculty member is tenured, often leads some faculty members to treat students (whether graduate or undergraduate) as indentured servants, or even worse, slaves.

I have personally known faculty members who have taken the thesis and/or dissertation of a student and, after some condensing and editing, listed themselves as first author of the eventual publication that resulted, with the student who wrote practically the entire thesis listed as the second author. I have also known other faculty members who, after assigning a graduate assistant (or an undergraduate student enrolled in an independent study) a topic to research, watched as the student conducted a thorough literature review around the topic under study, analyzed a wide variety of data (sometimes provided by the professor, oftentimes not), then wrote up the results for a paper; after the student had finished these efforts, with minimal guidance from the professor, the professor then contributed a methodology section (often lifted from a previous document he or she had written that described the data that was used for both studies) and gave the student ideas for a conclusion. After the process was over and the faculty member edited the work closely, the faculty member became first author on the publication.

I do not believe that most (or even many) faculty members are so egotistical that they must be listed as lead author for every piece that they coauthor to maintain some type of demagogue status in their psyche. I do believe, however, that many university faculty members often forget how influential they are in both a student's career and his/her professional development. As such, in their quest for the prestige, fame, and perhaps promotion and grant dollars that come with a strong vita that has a number of lead-authored publications, they often step on everyone in their way without regard for feelings or, more importantly, the morality of the actions in which they engage. In my mind, it is important that we stop this trend and turn the page back to article authorship where the one who does the most is first author, and all other authors follow in the order of the proportion of the work they produced.

No doubt some of you are thinking "Sure, he's a tenured, full professor; it is easy for him to say in 2008 that this behavior is unacceptable because he has already survived the promotion and tenure minefield." I agree that it is *easier* for me to talk about this subject at this point in my career, but I still would not say that it is an easy subject to discuss. Some faculty members may disagree with my philosophy for a number of reasons; in fact, some may feel that if they were the principal investigator for a grant that provided the data for a project (the situation that creates author disorder most often, in my experience), then they should be first author for the most meaningful publication(s) that result from that article. I could not disagree more; the reasons for my strong feelings are detailed below.

First, the amount of work an individual puts forth writing a grant that brings funding to obtain data should not have a correlation with the order of authorship on an article that may result from that data. Having written a number of grant proposals for which I successfully gained funding (and having written at least that many that were not funded), I understand the hard work involved in grant writing. I also understand the tedium, minutiae, and tremendous amount of drudgery that go along with administering a grant after it is funded. Nevertheless, all that work may have little to do with a publication that comes about from grant-funded data. Often, paper (and sometimes book) ideas result from a "fresh set of eyes" that look at the data and develop new ideas about what types of projects might result from the extant data collected as part of that grant. Consequently, the *publication* that results from the grant data may have little to do with the original purpose of the grant. As such, unless the principal investigator does the most work on the subsequent article, he or she does not deserve (nor should feel entitled to have) lead authorship on a paper from that data.

Second, one of the reasons I am so vehement about this topic is the situation I am discussing here happened to me very early in my career. I came up with a research idea, approached a professor (Professor A) who had relevant data to test and, after successfully gaining his approval for the project, conducted a thorough literature review, estimated the results, and wrote up a discussion of those results. In the time it took me to complete that process, another professor (Professor B) had heard about our project and wanted to be involved. Because of his position, Professor B felt it would be better for him and his research if he were listed as the first author, although he had done little on the project. When the article was submitted to a journal, and the order of authorship appeared with Professor B listed as lead author, I was furious. After talking with other professors, however, I decided that because I was almost finished with my Ph.D. (and because any debate had potential to create funding difficulties for a number of people), I would not protest too loudly and would use that experience as a moral compass for my career. I have done my best to do so.

I have a number of recommendations to reduce this problem of author disorder found so often in academia. These recommendations are discussed below.

1. **Order of authorship should carry less weight than it currently does for tenure and/or promotion.** In my opinion this current policy is the single greatest cause of author disorder. In those situations of which I am aware where author disorder has occurred, practically all revolved around the need for faculty members to obtain tenure, promotion, or a stronger vita so they could be a bigger player in the grant game. If faculty were told upon their initial employment that lead authorship of a work carried no more weight than second- or third-authorship, then faculty members would be less inclined to worry about author order.

2. **More weight should be given to student-co-authored publications in the promotion and tenure process.** Most (but certainly not all) university faculty members will tell you that the reason they became university professors was, in some shape, form, or fashion, to work with students. Couple that knowledge with the fact that students, particularly undergraduates, rarely care about the pedigree of faculty members as long as they are knowledgeable of the subject they are teaching and do so in an entertaining fashion, and it is hard to find the logic in the current state of most universities where student-authored publications carry equal weight with all other publications. If co-authorship with students were promoted and given greater weight than publications in which faculty members wrote with one another, faculty members would be less likely to engage in author disorder. In fact, this change might have two beneficial effects: reducing author disorder and *increasing* the chances that faculty members would actively seek students with whom they could co-author. Both of these situations would make the university a setting more in tune with what it was originally designed for—a place where students could receive a broad-based education from experts in their fields of study.

3. **Authorship should be established early—other professors may be able to control the egomaniacs where students could not.** Some would argue that the first two recommendations are currently unrealistic; while that view may be or seem true, the current university culture should not dissuade us from trying to make the university a more ethical place in which to work. In the interim, however, a step that needs to be taken immediately is that students need to know that when they work with faculty, faculty members do not naturally inherit lead authorship of any product that is produced. It is our job as university faculty members not only to make sure that students know that author disorder is unacceptable, but to proactively prevent author disorder from occurring.

One step in that direction is that all faculty members need to make a conscious effort to discuss authorship order with students prior to the work of any project in which we collaborate with students. From my own experience, students will never know that this discussion needs to take place until it is too late for the discussion and the faculty member has already assumed lead authorship of the article in question. Certainly, for student theses and dissertations, all faculty members should let the student know that he or she will be lead author on any product that results from the collaboration involved in creating the product adapted from the thesis or dissertation. Additionally, when students work on projects with faculty outside of the thesis or dissertation, this discussion also needs to take place, as students often play a major role in these projects as well. My own unwritten rule is that if the student is involved in the project at any level other than a bare minimum, that student precedes my own name in authorship. While I do not expect other faculty to adopt this standard, acknowledgement of the need to resist author disorder will make faculty more cognizant of this problem.

In closing, I reiterate that my own greatest joy in teaching occurs when I work with a student who begins a project with little confidence in his or her writing and research ability. Through the research process, the student realizes he or she really can work as a coauthor, collaborator, and a colleague, and end the project with much greater confidence in his or her abilities than before. Reducing author disorder is one way that we can ensure more students and faculty members are able to experience the joys of that process.

David C. May
Eastern Kentucky University

Discovery and Encouraging Scholarship

I strive to encourage enthusiasm and interest in research and scholarly efforts and did not realize, until recently, that I had found a way to "get the process started" with my master's level students. By searching for subtle signs of their interest in a particular issue or topic in their assignments and projects, I can encourage further exploration that can frequently lead to a variety of scholarship pursuits. As an example, in a recent fall semester I was particularly impressed by the repeated references and excellent online discussion board forum postings of one student about the general topic of Caregiver Stress and the specific issue of the elderly caring for family members. Subsequently, I went back and read her previous week's work and found a depth of content along with a "voice" of passion in the subject that was both remarkable and an obvious avenue for me to pursue to encourage her further exploration and sharing her findings with her colleagues, both in written and verbal formats. I contacted her by email and set up a time for a convenient telephone conference to discuss potential integration of her interest with our current Advanced Health Assessment course. During the ensuing weeks of the semester she not only readily discussed with me (and her course colleagues) the reasons behind her interest in the subject (a much admired grandmother who had cared for ailing family members) but also her interest in research and finding and using evidence based resources to provide a solid foundation for care planning for caregivers and their families. Exploring peer reviewed resources for specific course projects and assignments was one of her personal major priorities and objectives, along with sharing her findings with her colleagues on our online discussion board forums and improving her writing and presentation skills. During each discussion (online, in person, and on the telephone) I provided didactic information about how to select appropriate professional and scholarly resources, improving written and verbal communication while at the same encouraging her to look at the patient's entire family, home and work environments. Simultaneously, she integrated body system assessment (normals versus abnormals) so she could assure completion of our course objectives while exploring her individual research interests. She was quite enthusiastic throughout the entire semester and quite willing to not only focus on the specific course assignments but also "thrilled to be able to also pursue and include her own interests as well." She subsequently went above and beyond the assignments and projects and examined (through exploration of peer-reviewed resources) the psychosocial aspects of the caregiver and patient in a variety of settings (in the hospital, nursing home, community-based adult day care, and Alzheimer's care centers).

As a result of our work together during this initial core course we mutually agreed to work together as faculty mentor and student in her Professional Scholarship course (master's level students are required to pursue a 1 hour Professional Scholarship course and are paired with faculty members who have similar research and professional areas/ topics of interest as the student). Her continued exploration and active pursuit of evidence-based information evolved to include the perceptions and opinions through face-to-face interviews with community-based health-care providers who provided additional insight into the "real-world" of care giving in elderly populations. Her enthusiasm and discovery processes during her research project were a joy to watch. Her ultimate course outcomes were outstanding and included providing her colleagues in outpatient settings with an assessment tool of caregiver stress. Her assessment tool along with a prototype for practice guidelines for implementation in community-based settings provided not only objective tools for immediate use but also an excellent example of how scholarship can be put into action and positive changes can be made through scholarly pursuits. What began as a personal interest became an identifiable product and produced a remarkable and exciting scholarly product and potentially a lifelong interest and career pursuit for the student. FYI – She currently is working on developing a research project with another graduate student – in the area of Caregiver Stress – of course!

Subsequently, I have had the privilege of repeating this type of professional scholarship mentoring relationship several times with master's level students. Frequently, the journey together began in much the same way, with the realization that the student was repeatedly mentioning (usually timidly and hesitantly in the beginning) a particular topic or issue. Identification of: (1) recurrent "themes" or threads in student coursework, (2) repeated or related questions in a focused, particular area, (3) coursework or online postings that always seem to "come back to" a particular area of interest, or perhaps(4) an excellent "over to top" assignment completed in a particular area when all other assignments have been just average are just a few of the subtle signs students give us that provide insight into what might spark their interest not only in specific course content but research processes in general. I have been able, a few times, to pick up on their subtle clues and encourage the pursuit of THEIR individual interests (not to the point of ignoring other assignments but shifting the focus a bit to include their burning and underlying passions). If (and this is a big "if") we, as educators, pick up on the subtle signs of interest our students display, perhaps we can fan the "spark" into becoming a "fire" and facilitate discovery and development of their own personal and lifelong scholarly habits and tools.

Wrennah L. Gabbert
Texas Tech University

_____

The Slightly-Less Blind Leading the Blind: Faculty-Student Teaching Research Group

"It is the true nature of mankind to learn from mistakes, not from example." Fred Hoyle

I was the reluctant hold-out to beginning a collaborative faculty-student research interest group. My esteemed colleagues, with their long publication track record, embraced the model years ago. I, on the other hand, figured that the Publication Train had long since left the station for me because I lacked the razor-like focus necessary to succeed in this form of academic scholarship. My publication track record was therefore limited to occasional non-validated pedagogical soapboxes in our faculty newsletter.

Despite these fears, a group of five dedicated doctoral psychology students and I began a teaching research group. These students, who ranged from 1st year to 4th year in their doctorate studies, were diverse in their professional interests, but united in one respect: our passion for and commitment to teaching. The group also ranged in experience regarding teaching from experienced teachers to those teaching for the first time to those who hoped to someday enter the profession. We met once every two weeks and also communicated regularly via email to review drafts and process ideas. Participation in the group was voluntarily, but participants were asked to make a commitment to be fully working group members after sampling a few meetings. We met at a mutually convenient time, after our morning classes and before our evening ones.

Although we didn't intend for the teaching research group to mirror the traditional "scholarship of investigation," in some ways, it did. We got excited about important questions in teaching: which elements and activities of our teaching are working and which are not? what components at our quasi-learner-centered style of teaching contribute to students' learning? To answer these questions, we split the workload according to each member's skills and interests. Some members found and shared relevant articles (see below for a few examples); some created an applied research design that would yield usable data but still be practical for our busy lives; some ran statistics and translated their meaning for the rest of us. Our study designs were simple: we created supplemental course evaluations and administered them across instructors, courses, and programs (undergraduate, graduate, adult learners). We collected data that was both quantitative (Likert-scale) and qualitative (open-ended questions). We worked with the university's ethics committee to ensure we were following all ethical guidelines in data collection.

What we found, gathered through approximately 75 supplemental course evaluations, is that students are overwhelmingly positive about courses taking a more learner-centered approach. They are able to recognize and appreciate the key tenets of learner-centered teaching in their classroom, including shifting the balance of power to students; returning the responsibility of learning to students; changing the role of teacher to co-learner; using content as a way to encourage thinking about deeper issues; and utilizing assessment measures to promote learning instead of just assigning grades (Weimer, 2002). They attribute their learning in the classroom to many of these principles, but mostly to the feeling of trust they sense the professor has in them. This data has helped informed our teaching practices and has directly contributed to our increasing understanding of what good teaching is. For example, we learned that students handle the "return of power" tenet better when they have to commit to an early semester work plan instead of having an "ultimate deadline" for completion of work towards the end of the semester. In other words, for learner-centered ideas to work, students need to feel not only a strong sense of trust, but some scaffolding and structured support that helps them succeed.

This same sense of trust, mentioned above as being important to students, permeates our research interest group. We learned from each other how to strengthen our skills in teaching and research. We saw the intimate connection between scholarship and teaching and how they inform each other. We held each other accountable with deadlines and tasks. We edited each other's work, supported each other when we received rejection letters, and pushed each other to succeed. And because none of us knew exactly what we were doing, we unintentionally created a safe atmosphere where it was ok to make mistakes, even colossal ones, which we ("I" is actually a better pronoun choice) did, including making a technological error and sending in only half of our proposal to speak at a prestigious conference and misunderstanding a communication of a rejection notice as an acceptance and excitedly sharing the news with a group, only to crush spirits later. Our naïveté usually worked well for us: we had no idea of how likely failure was, so we attempted to publish and present at a variety of venues with equal abandon. We learned to email editors and conference organizers for assistance and repeatedly found helpful individuals with a willingness to mentor our publication-free group. These individuals provided us with feedback, including how to make our data collection process stronger (collect data from across professors) and how to ground our tips in current research.

What began as an overt effort to lengthen our vitae became instead a collaborative effort to strengthen our skills. We wanted to not only "look good" to the professional world; we wanted to know what we were talking about. We began to understand the Scholarship of Teaching and Learning field and how our little group fit into a broader universe of ideas. As a result, we have never been more excited about, or informed of, our teaching. Research became a less distant, forbidden word and instead an exciting, tangible, yet muddy reality. And we are still meeting, learning, laughing, trying, failing, and sometimes succeeding, less so because of my leadership than because of the hard-working, talented, skilled, thoughtful team of students working with me. Thus far, our little-research-group-that-could has had two national presentations and five state presentations accepted, along with three peer-reviewed journal articles pending. Not bad work for a virgin group of academicians.

This article provides little in the way of concrete suggestions of how to create a research interest group, but perhaps it provides something more: inspiration and some borrowed confidence that we are all capable scholars who have something to offer. Publishing doesn't have to be grand and perfect; real world and muddy are ok, too. And one can be a scholar and still be a decent human being who has a life outside academia.

References

Bilimoria, D. & Wheeler, J.V. (1995). Learning-centered education: a guide to resources and implementation. Journal of Management Education, 29(3), 402-428.

Daley, B.J. (2003). A case for learner-centered teaching and learning. New Directions for Adult and Continuing Education, 98, 23-30.

Weimer, M. (2002). Learner-centered teaching: five key changes to practice. San Francisco, CA: Jossey-Bass.

DeDe Wohlfarth
Jody Pimentel
Laura Gabel
Jess Bennett
Dan Sheras
Beth Simon
Spalding University

_____

Community Newspaper Research Projects Benefit Students, Newspapers and Professor

Like most professors who teach at institutions with heavy teaching loads, I have difficulty finding time for research while also fulfilling my teaching and service obligations. A solution that works for me and pays dividends for students and newspapers is to incorporate a research project into a required capstone course.

Since 1991, each time Community Journalism, the capstone course for journalism majors, has been offered, the class has been paired with a community newspaper to conduct research for the paper. Originally, the projects were funded by the Kentucky Press Association as a member service and restricted to locally owned weekly newspapers. A secondary purpose was to recruit journalism graduates to work for community newspapers. After eight projects, that funding — $1,000 per class – was no longer available. I approached other newspapers in Eastern's service area and have had little trouble finding newspapers to participate and to pay for the projects. Through 2008, 14 projects have been completed. (I conducted 12 of them and two colleagues supervised one project each while I was on sabbatical leaves.)

Here's how the projects work:

Before the semester, I find a publisher/editor who is willing to have his or her newspaper serve as the class project. I meet with the publisher/editor to determine preliminary goals for the project and to begin formulating a concurrent research project I may want to conduct. The newspaper's goals and my instructional objectives for the class must be compatible.

Students spend the first part of the course learning the characteristics of good community newspapers, reading and critiquing the client newspaper, shadowing the staff, creating a profile of the newspaper's community, and setting final goals for the project.

I provide a crash course in basic research methods, and students develop a plan for achieving the newspaper's goals. Most projects have used mail surveys of randomly selected subscribers and non-subscribers. One used a random telephone survey of community residents. Recent projects used online surveys to reach readers of the newspaper's Web site in addition to mail surveys of print edition subscribers. Students have also surveyed advertisers and newspaper employees, conducted accuracy surveys with people named in articles, and interviewed local officials. Students develop questionnaires, pretest them, choose a sample, distribute questionnaires, compile and analyze data (with some statistical help from me), and write a final report, which includes not only survey results but also interviews with newspaper staff, critiques of the paper and recommendations based on the research findings. All students have a hand in writing, editing, and designing the report, thereby showcasing their journalism skills. Each student receives a copy of the report, which is often more than 100 pages. For the final exam, students make a presentation to the newspaper staff and distribute copies of the printed report.

I've found the projects to be an effective way to expose students to all aspects of community journalism and to give them a chance to conduct meaningful research. The projects also benefit the newspapers, providing them with research data their staffs might not otherwise have the time or resources to gather. Some newspapers have made important decisions based on the students' research findings and recommendations. The projects are also bargains for the newspapers because they pay only for the actual costs of the project, including copying and printing, postage, travel for the students and the professor, food for out-of-class work sessions, and a luncheon at which the results are presented. Most recent projects have been completed for less than $2,000.

Students rate the class very high on evaluations, and the professional journalists who evaluate the projects give the students high marks. At least one student got a job specifically because of the research skills she learned, and many of the students have put those skills to work in their jobs as journalists—both in conducting their own studies and in evaluating research done by others. Students like knowing their work contributes to knowledge about audiences of community newspapers and the newspapers' relationships with their communities. Almost all of the students will work for community newspapers for at least part of their careers.

The projects have also been an effective way to increase my research productivity. My first refereed paper from the projects was an overview of how the projects work, which was presented to a national symposium of community newspaper publishers/editors and academics who study community journalism. Since then, I've published two articles, presented four additional refereed papers, written and presented a commissioned paper, contributed to a publication on using the community in the classroom that was distributed at a national journalism educators' convention, and participated in a panel at a national meeting on conducting community journalism research.

I've gathered data for my own research in several ways. With the approval of both the newspaper and the students, I've added a few questions to the student-developed questionnaires. Combining the responses to those questions with other survey data has provided the basis for some papers. I also conducted a longitudinal study, combining data from two projects with the same newspaper with content analysis of issues published in the weeks before the readership surveys were conducted. I credit the classes' contributions in my papers and articles.

While these projects are newspaper specific, the concept could be adapted for use in other disciplines. Newspaper publishers are similar to other small business owners who want to learn more about their customers. I have had public relations campaigns and writing classes conduct surveys for non-profit organizations that wanted to measure public awareness of their programs. While those projects did not result in any scholarly works on my part, they provided lessons I have incorporated in the community journalism projects. Among the lessons: verify students' work and get written permission from the client to use the research findings in scholarly works.

The bottom line: These projects integrate scholarship with both teaching and service and work for everyone involved.

Elizabeth K. Hansen
Eastern Kentucky University

Collaborating with Students in the Arts & Humanities

Over the years we have collaborated on 99% of our publications, but almost never with students. In fact, in the arts & humanities faculty and students rarely collaborate. We know this kind of working together is prevalent in the sciences, but we're not sure why the practice is shunned in our discipline. Perhaps we're at fault for not trying to do it more often.

But we have done it. For a report on how effective one such collaboration was, see our *It Works for Us, Collaboratively!* (pp. 98-100). Basically our collaborations with students have come down to two venues, conference presentations and publications. Over the years we have also helped students write papers for various events, such as campus showcases, but we were more editors than mentors or collaborators. Nonetheless, we would suggest a few guidelines for collaborating with students in the arts & humanities.

One, **actively seek out opportunities to present with students**. Most universities have on-campus conferences, and most disciplines have a state-wide conference—these are perfect venues for allowing students to get their feet wet. Some faculty take students to these conferences, but rarely do they co-present.

Two, **assign the kind of papers in your classes that are suitable for conferences and publications**. In our junior-level American Lit classes, we culminate the semester with scholarly notes. If the notes are fairly good, we have the students send them off to journals in the field. And, yes, some of our students have published these notes, even though they are competing with tenure-track faculty. However, sometimes students have good ideas and no support in their essays, while other times they brush against the tip of an iceberg, an iceberg in which you catch a glimpse of a worthwhile idea. Why not collaborate on these essays? Think of the learning that takes place when you guide a student from idea to article or help the student research proper support for an essentially good idea.

Three, **when you have good students, perhaps in a seminar or grad class, propose writing a group-authored article with them.** If nothing else, these students could do the necessary research. Other times you could break the essay down into areas (e.g., "Group Alpha, you take Act I ..."), and then your second function would be to pull the work of these research and writing communities into one well organized article. According to a recent report in the *Chronicle of Higher Education*, the number one thing businesses are looking for in our students is the ability to do teamwork. Wouldn't this mentored group paper help students learn how to function as a team? Right now, for instance, as co-directors of the Teaching & Learning Center, we have a grad student assigned to us. In the past two months Ben has demonstrated the ability to research and to organize that research (he's in organizational psychology), so we're getting ready to start an article on faculty development with him. Admittedly the project might not work, but it's an experiment worth trying.

Hal Blythe
Charlie Sweet
Eastern Kentucky University

The Consultant Role: Application of Organizational Behavior Concepts Through Service

The goal of the project is to link the concepts discussed in class to the real world in a meaningful way. The primary objective is to apply class material to a real-life challenge in a case analysis format. Students choose a non-profit organization with which to work, integrating the student into the community through service learning. This provides students with meaningful contacts in the community as well as objective experience in working with professionals and residents of the community on a common goal. The activity will be determined by the non-profit organization and will be *15 hours* in length. Signature verification of hours completed is required.

The organization should **not** be a place of paid employment for the student. If a family member or friend works for the organization, the student should not work with that individual. Because the experience works best in an objective setting, I require students to work within "target populations" typically outside of students' comfort zones. I specifically require that the non-profit agency chosen must serve the **Mental Retarda-**

tion and Developmental Disability (MRDD) population and provide several points of contact.

The first step is for students to identify a situation within the organization in which they believe improvement is both necessary and possible and is addressed in a chapter covered in class (for example, communication or stress). It need not involve a lot of people nor an extremely complex problem, but it should address a situation which presently has a problem which prevents maximum efficiency and/or effectiveness.

The Analysis of Organizational Behavior Paper is designed to help students demonstrate their understanding of the organization as well as the social issue(s) they strive to ease. Using *documented sources,* the paper should include the following information:

I.	Name and purpose of the organization.	
II.	Problem Recognition:	Organizational challenge discussed in class or text.
III.	Setting Objectives:	What will be accomplished through problem reconciliation?
IV.	Group Identification:	Specify who is affected.
V.	Generation of Options:	At least 2 options to reconcile the problem objectives.
VII.	Option Selection:	Which option is the "best" choice and why?
VIII.	Option Implementation:	How would the solution be implemented in the organization?
IX.	Bibliography. Using *APA format*, provide a **minimum of 5 sources** in reference to the organization and/or the defined problem. *No more than 2* web pages may be used as references.	

The Analysis of Organizational Behavior Paper is assessed using the following rubric:

Performance Element	Criteria	3 = Excellent 2 = Average 1 = Needs Improvement		
Name and purpose of the organization	1. Organization name identified.	3	2	1
	2. Organizational purpose identified	3	2	1
	3. Citation(s) used in documentation of organizational purpose	3	2	1
Problem Recognition	1. Identified whether problem is one of communication, stress, etc.	3	2	1
	2. At least one specific example of the identified problem is given.	3	2	1
Setting Objectives	1. Expectations are clearly stated about what will be accomplished by the proposed solution(s).	3	2	1
	2. There are measureable outcomes that will show the proposed change, e.g., fewer sick days, less paper used per month.	3	2	1
Group Identification	1. Identify all groups directly affected by the identified problem	3	2	1
	2. Identify all groups indirectly affected by the identified problem	3	2	1
Generation of Options	At least two, differentiable solutions to the identified problem presented	3	2	1
Option Evaluation	1. Each of the options is evaluated according to the objective set in element 3, including pros and cons of each	3	2	1
	2. The evaluations are supported by logical reasoning.			
	3. Citation(s) are used in documentation of option evaluation	3	2	1
		3	2	1
Option Selection	1. The recommendations grow logically out of the option evaluation.	3	2	1
	2. The recommendations are clearly stated and explained	3	2	1
Option Implementation	1. The recommendations are specific enough to serve as the basis for decisions by management	3	2	1
	2. The stages of implementation are clearly stated and explained	3	2	1
References	1. At least five sources are cited.	3	2	1
	2. All sources in the bibliography are referenced in the Analysis of Organizational Behavior Paper.	3	2	1
	3. APA format is correctly used.	3	2	1
Professionalism	1. The paper looks neat, crisp, and professional.	3	2	1
	2. The paper is stapled.	3	2	1
	3. Spelling and Grammar.	3	2	1

Hints
1) This tip has been very effective in helping students apply course concepts in a meaningful way by allowing them to work in an objective setting. Through the exercise, students feel as though they are developing skills while acting as consultants and achieving a better understanding of the intricacies of problem reconciliation.

2) I have successfully utilized this tip in my sophomore level Organizational Behavior classes.

Leslie Elrod
University of Cincinnati

Can We Make Group Work Work?

For years we have used team based assignments in our classes and have been frustrated with our evaluation method. Like many, we incorporated peer assessment of group contributions into our grading system, but were often disappointed by the results. Typically, students were overly generous, assigning inflated scores to their peers. We had no system for students to offer anonymous written feedback, resulting in a missed opportunity for students to learn how others perceived their group contributions. Each semester at least a few members complained to the instructor about other students' work, but refused to confront the issue in their groups. Sometimes, we detected in the final product a high variance in members' contributions. Often the final product indicated a lack of team work or extreme differences in effort put forth by each student. Furthermore, students often complained about group work generally on their end-of-the-semester evaluations. Still, we were committed to group learning and were determined to make it work.

In spring 2008, we implemented a modified version of the peer assessment method offered by L. Dee Fink (2002). Fink's system involved soliciting numerical scores from each group member about the contributions of other group members, but allowed only a finite number of points to be distributed across the group. If everyone contributed equally, an equal number of points would be distributed. However, if the evaluator believed that someone contributed above the rest, points must be subtracted from another member. This system was designed to prompt students to consider more carefully how to distribute a scarce number of points. Peer evaluators would then provide written explanations of their scores. Students filled out the peer evaluations online using Excel spreadsheets.

The Class and Assignments

The class was an undergraduate social work class of 22 students called *Human Behavior and the Social Environment*. Class members were sophomores and juniors majoring in social work; some were acquainted and some were strangers. Early in the semester, students formed groups to complete two graded assignments: (1) to lead one class session relating to a chapter in our text and(2) to research aspects of a particular life stage, (childhood, adolescence, etc.), interview a person from the life stage, and write a group paper about their observations. Students were asked to evaluate themselves and group members in five categories: Overall participation, Leadership/ Helping, Quality of Work, Share of Workload, Timeliness of work.

The Research

Our method for documenting students' perceptions of Fink's peer assessment system involved two phases. Early in the semester students were given a short Likert Scale survey to rate aspects of their previous experience with group projects, such as how much they enjoyed group work, how effective professors had been in facilitating their work, and how fairly they thought group work had been graded, along with additional written comments.. At the end of the semester students responded to the same questions to measure any changes. In order to collect additional qualitative data, a graduate student assistant conducted a focus group interview to explore students' perceptions of the effectiveness and value of the peer-evaluation system.

Results

In the survey given at the beginning of the semester, students reported primarily positive experiences with group work: For example, 84% reported that group work had positively contributed to their education and 68% agreed they enjoyed group work. The majority perceived that the workload was usually shared evenly (74%). However, students seemed to wish for more instructor guidance, with only 53% percent agreeing that professors guided group work well. In written comments, several students noted that the one-grade-for-all system seemed unfair, while others expected that one or two students typically completed most of the work while the rest contributed only when necessary.

After experiencing our system of peer evaluation, students' views of group work were even more positive, with reported enjoyment increasing about 10% and their view of group work's value increasing by 11%. Interestingly, their view of the professor's role remained constant, with only 53% agreeing with the statement: "My instructors have been good at guiding the group and evaluating progress during the working phase." In the post-semester focus group interview, students pointed to both strengths and limitations in the peer evaluation method. They recognized ways in which the system could potentially stretch group members beyond their natural inclinations, especially in the area of leadership. Some students noted that they benefited from this system because it encouraged them to be more honest and objective in their evaluations, especially when dealing with those who did not pull their weight. Some even noted that the practice of giving and receiving honest evaluations offered meaningful preparation for their professional roles

On the other hand, the students expressed reservations about key aspects of the evaluation system. Most commonly, the finite number of points available for evaluating the members of the group was questioned. This system bothered many students since they could only award higher points to one person by taking points away from others. Several students even recommended using some sort of a bonus system so that a person could be rewarded for exceptional contributions without penalizing the others. Some found the combination of assigning scores and providing written comments tedious. Others questioned how effectively the grading system motivated the individual members of the group by pointing out that negative evaluations could be counterproductive if the comments were received between scheduled assignments or if they could guess who had made which comment. Still, one student commented that she appreciated receiving the written comments more than the numerical scores. The numbers seemed impersonal and vague, while the comments offered specific advice or commendation.

In the end, the majority of the comments offered point to the overall effectiveness of this system for soliciting honest and useful assessments, not only for more accurate assignments of grades, but for students' growth in group work skills. Perhaps the most telling comment we received was that many of the students said that they would recommend the system to other professors, particularly those who assign group projects for large classes.

Conclusion

Overall, our study found that Fink's peer-evaluation method was beneficial. While some students found it tedious and somewhat uncomfortable to evaluate their peers in such detail, the majority recognized its heuristic value and effectiveness. The system's ability to promote honest evaluations, to provide motivation for the social loafers, and to allow instructors to gain a better sense of how the groups worked together proved its effectiveness in making group work work.

Reference

Fink, L. D. (2002) Calculating peer evaluation scores: Appendix B; in L. Michaelson, A. B. Knight, L. D. Fink, *Team based learning: A transformative use of small groups;* Westport, CT, Praeger, pp. 233-240.

T. Laine Scales
Christopher M. Rios
Baylor University

www.ingramcontent.com/pod-product-compliance
Lightning Source LLC
Chambersburg PA
CBHW080556090426
42735CB00016B/3254